JEAN FROST

Jackets

Fabric, fit & finish for today's knits

another publication of  BOOKS

Jean Frost Jackets
PUBLISHED BY XRX BOOKS

PUBLISHER
Alexis Yiorgos Xenakis

EDITOR
Elaine Rowley

EDITORIAL ASSISTANT
Sue Nelson

KNITTING EDITOR
Gail McHugh

COPY EDITOR
Holly Brunner

GRAPHIC DESIGNER
Bob Natz

PHOTOGRAPHER
Alexis Yiorgos Xenakis

FASHION & TECHNICAL EDITOR
Rick Mondragon

PHOTO STYLIST
Bev Nimon

DIRECTOR, PUBLISHING SERVICES
David Xenakis

PRODUCTION DIRECTOR
Dennis Pearson

BOOK PRODUCTION MANAGER
Natalie Sorenson

DIGITAL COLOR SPECIALIST
Jason Bittner

PRODUCTION
Everett Baker

TECHNICAL ILLUSTRATIONS
Jay Reeve
Carol Skallerud

SECOND PRINTING, 2003;
FIRST PUBLISHED IN USA IN 2003 BY XRX, INC.

COPYRIGHT © 2003 XRX, INC.

ISBN 1-893762-15-7

Produced by XRX, Inc.
PO Box 1525
Sioux Falls, SD 57101-1525
605.338.2450

JEAN FROST

Jackets

Fabric, fit & finish for today's knits

Why knit a jacket?

When women first entered the business world, they dressed to fit in, not to stand out. Their suits resembled the men's: same fabrics, same colors, almost the same styles. Everyone looked the same. As women settled in, they began to show their individual style. At the same time, Giorgio Armani, Diane von Furstenberg, and Karl Lagerfeld at Chanel introduced a less-structured style of dress. The softer tailoring in their suit jackets and coordinated separates gave us just what we still want: style, individuality, and comfort.

The knitted jacket builds on this tradition. Wear it to work, to play, or just because. The knitted jacket is welcome at any event and all occasions. It pairs with skirts or slacks, works over dresses and even jeans. It does not wrinkle and is easy to care for—a real boon for today's woman!

When you knit your own jacket, you are in complete control. Combine color, texture, or fiber for beautiful and unique fabrics. The options are limitless. A jacket is an investment piece, no matter how small or large the price, so think classic, think quality. These styles are timeless.

If your life is full and it seems easiest to fit in small knitting projects, why not think of a jacket as several small projects? One back, two fronts, two sleeves, and perhaps a collar or a set of pockets: your sense of satisfaction grows with the completion of each. And before you know it, you've added a jacket to your wardrobe.

When your jacket is noticed—and it will be—you can proudly say, "Thank you, I knit it myself."

Jean Frost

Always in style:

Jean Frost wearing Sanquar.

Fisherman's Wharf. The Golden Gate Bridge. Cable cars. Storied Alcatraz. The knitting universe seemed to come to life for this English major-turned-Knitter's Magazine publisher at The National Needlework Association (TNNA) show in San Francisco. Amidst the swirl of color, texture, and people was an elegant woman with short dark hair, a striking hand knit sweater, dark pants, and, it turned out, a degree in English Literature. Jean Frost's petite stature and smiling face reminded me of my favorite aunt Kanella, who used to cut up her old wool skirts and sew them into short pants for me. When she wasn't helping me climb her fig tree for figs, that is.

"I love to sew, and I have a fig tree in my backyard!" Jean said. I knew I was going to like this woman, but how could I have known then that one day I would be writing the introduction for her book?

"It was so much fun going from booth to booth at that TNNA," Jean recalls. "All that yarn! I was wearing a sweater I had designed using Cheryl Schaefer's 'Shoestring.' Which was nothing more than tie-dyed shoestrings! How ingenious was that? I was walking along, and in the background I heard someone say, 'You've got my yarn!' I wasn't holding any yarn in my hands, so I didn't think that was directed at me, and kept going. But suddenly someone grabbed my hand: it was Cheryl. 'Your sweater is knitted out of my yarn,' she said. 'I like the pattern. Can I buy it?' She did, and that's what got me started."

But Jean's design career started before that fortuitous encounter with one of the handpaint world's premier artists. "In junior high," Jean says, "a friend had a beautiful collection of sweaters. I admired them from afar, but never said a thing. Until one day, I couldn't stand it anymore and told her how much I loved the sweater she had on. She told me she knitted it.

"I had never seen anybody knit before, had no idea how to do it. But I thought, if she could do it, I could do it. So I went home and asked my mom if she knew how to knit. She said yes, and I said, 'Please teach me'. And she did, rather reluctantly at first, because she didn't think I'd stay with it. With one ball of yarn and a pair of needles, she taught me to cast on, knit, purl, increase, decrease, bind off—everything I needed to know. And she made me knit that ball of yarn over and over again until my knitting was absolutely perfect.

an Introduction

"Then she gave me enough money to buy the yarn to make a sweater: it cost two dollars and fifty cents. I wore it everywhere and still have it! That was a time when everyone was making Sloppy Joe sweaters: crew neck, round collar, puffy sleeves, blousy things with buttoned-down fronts. Not at all fancy, but they were the rage—at least in my town, Louisville, Kentucky. I think I made about twelve—the same sweater, in different colors."

When the Sloppy Joe craze was over, Jean discovered Irish knits. She had studied English and Art in college, married a young doctor, and had her first child. "When my first son was born," she says, "I discovered cables—and started making Irish sweaters for everybody. When more children came along I started knitting clothes for myself because they were affordable: cocktail dresses, skirts, suits, sweaters—anything I could think of. And I designed them all. "With a husband and four children, where did she find the time to do all that knitting? "All my kids were swimmers," Jean says, "so there were lots of swim meets and practice before and after school. So I took my knitting along. The kids swam, I knitted!

"I've always approached my knitting from my perspective as a seamstress. I've always tailored my own clothes, and I translated that into my designing. The nice thing about knitting is that it drapes and hugs the body. Unlike woven fabric that you have to dart and cut into shape, knitting is so flexible. You could say that what I try to do is think of producing a knitted fabric rather than a knitted object.

"That's exactly what happened with my Fairfield jacket [page 18]. Are you familiar with Belleek china from Ireland? I have a vase that looks like woven wicker with a scalloped edge on top. That's where the inspiration for the lace collar came from. The basket weave stitch, of course, imitates the basket weave of the china. The pottery is a translucent cream color, so that was reflected in the choice of yarn as well. One day I was looking at the vase and thought, I can knit that—and I did.

"Another time the process began with a quilted jacket. I thought, Why can't I do that in knitting? For my pattern stitch I used what is called pencil quilting, a narrow row of knitted stitches with a purl stitch in between, a sort of mock ribbing. Quilted jackets seem to always have a leaf or flower motif, so I took that idea and inserted the lace leaf

From top: Fairfield, Hanover, Siobhan

decoration on the bottom of the sleeves and body. Hanover [page 72] is one of my favorites.

"Sometimes it's the color that gets me started. Look at Siobhan [page 78]. That emerald green made me think of leaves, so the lace leaf motif was a natural choice. The bottom of the jacket—an elongated leaf—creates a peplum."

Whatever the inspiration, the underlying influence in Jean Frost's work is a legendary French designer who, Jean says, reinvented women's clothes. "At a time of all those buttons and hooks & eyes, Coco Chanel created fashionable clothes that were comfortable; that you could get around in; that you didn't have to have someone help you get into! (Chanel actually started making clothes out of the knitted jersey used to make men's underwear.) In my mind, her piece de resistance was what we call the Chanel jacket, that revolutionary design that appeared after World War II.

"Chanel jackets were something everybody wanted to wear. They were simple, dressy or not, and they looked elegant—not just on Coco but on everybody else. There are a number of jackets in the book that show her influence: Gloucester [page 68] is basically a Chanel jacket. The Trilling [page 22] is another Chanel-inspired four-pocket design that I saw in a photograph.

"But the first jacket I made for the book was the Sanquar [page 54] out of Cheryl Schaefer's yarn. It's white with blue multicolored yarn featured on the borders. My daughters, Dawn and Holly, both being in business and traveling, remembered my knitted suits—the fact that they pack well and don't wrinkle—and said to me, 'Why don't you start making jackets again?'

"It took a little over a week to knit the Sanquar. And soon, the other designs followed. It took me about a year to knit them all. As the yarns chosen by the XRX editors arrived, I'd go to work: I'd try a stitch pattern I wanted to work with. If it looked good, I'd go ahead; if not, I'd try something else. I've always had a feel for what the yarn can do, but sometimes I'd discard five or six stitch patterns before picking the one I liked. And all the while, I kept thinking of simpler designs that beginners could do, like the Somerset jacket.

From top: Trilling, Gloucester, Boylston

"Whether sporty or dressy, cotton, wool, or a blend, what I want is a jacket that's nicely tailored and has a certain elegance—something that flatters, that's just right. And while the emphasis might be on the background stitch pattern, the edges, or collar—invariably, the sleeves are set in. A set-in sleeve is such a simple construction, and this is one of the reasons I think my jackets look as tailored as they do.

"Details are also important. And you can put the emphasis where you want: on the edges, the body of the sweater, the collar. You work it all out as you go along. Make it a jacket you like to wear. After you see what goes into it, go out on your own and see what you can do. And if something doesn't work right, rip it out and try something else. At least you've learned something.

"Take the time to choose the right yarn, the right pattern, maybe even make some design changes to suit your personal style. Then you will not only find a creative outlet in your knitting—you can create something you feel proud of and look great in."

And with that, Jean heads out to the patio where, on this warm winter morning the plumerias are blooming, the birds are eating ripe red pyracantha berries, and the only thing that lets her know the season has changed are a few golden leaves on a potted plant. And that fig tree? "Oh," she says, "unfortunately I had to leave it behind in L.A. when I moved to the foothills of San Diego."

Well, Jean, we'll just have to visit my aunt Kanella's. I know you've got a great travel wardrobe.

— Alexis Xenakis

Sioux Falls, SD

Left: Jean Frost wearing Piedmont, above: Somerset

01

Newbury
page 2

02

Tremont
page 6

03

Somerset
page 10

04

Chardon
page 14

05

Fairfield
page 18

06

Trilling
page 22

07

Copley
page 26

08

Piedmont
page 30

09

Claridge
page 34

15
Stuart
page 60

16
Clarendon
page 64

17
Gloucester
page 68

18
Hanover
page 72

19
Siobhan
page 78

Contents

Newbury 01

This jacket is as easy to knit as it is to wear. The shape is straight and the stitches are simple: stockinette and seed. A narrow tie threaded through "buttonholes" at the V-neck fastens the fronts together. But the tie can be removed and replaced by a pin, should you wish. An attractive jacket that can be worn all most anywhere.

Women's M: BROWN SHEEP CO.
Naturespun - 8 balls #701 Stone

Newbury

Easy plus

LOOSE FIT

FINISHED measurements

Women's S (M, L, XL)
A *43 (46, 49, 51½)"*
B *20½ (21½, 24½, 26½)"*
C *28 (29¾, 31¼, 31¾)"*

10cm/4"

over Stockinette stitch

Light weight
1200 (1300, 1600, 1700) yds

3.25 mm/US 3
or size to obtain gauge

4 mm/US F

NOTES

1 See Techniques (page 96) for 3-needle bind-off, ssk, one-row buttonhole, lifted increase, and seam instructions. *2* Work edge sts at seam edges in Garter st (k every row). All increases and decreases are worked after the beginning edge st or before the ending edge st. *3* Slip all sts purlwise.

Seed pattern (over an even number of sts)
Row 1 (RS) *P1, k1; repeat from*.
Row 2 *K1, p1; repeat from*.

Seed pattern (over an odd number of sts)
Row 1 (RS) *P1, k1; repeat from*, end p1.
Row 2 *K1, p1; repeat from*, end k1.

BACK

Cast on 128 (134, 140, 150) sts. (RS) Work Seed pattern for 11 rows, knitting first and last st of every row for seam edge st. **Next row** (WS) K1, purl to last st, k1 **Next row** K. Repeat last 2 rows until Back measures 13 (14, 16, 17)", ending with a WS row.

Shape armhole

Bind off 10 sts at beginning of next 2 rows. **Decrease row** (RS) K1 (edge st), k2tog, work St st to last 3 sts, ssk, k1 (edge st)—2 sts decreased. Work Decrease row every RS row, 7 (7, 7, 9) more times, until 92 (98, 104, 110) sts remain. Work even until armhole measures 7 (7, 8, 9)", ending with a WS row. Place all sts on hold.

LEFT FRONT

Cast on 68 (74, 80, 84) sts. (RS) *K1 (side seam edge), work Row 1 of Seed pattern to 1 st remaining, slip the last st purlwise with yarn in front (front edge). **Next row** K1 (front edge), work Row 2 of Seed pattern to 1 st remaining, k1 (side seam edge). Repeat from* for a total of 11 rows. **Next row** (WS) K1, work 7 sts in Seed pattern (front band), purl to 1 st remaining, k1. **Next row** (RS) Knit to 8 sts remaining, work in Seed pattern for 7 sts, sl 1 with yarn in front. Repeat last two rows until Left Front measures 11 (12, 14, 15)", ending with a WS row.

Make buttonhole

Next row (RS) Knit to 8 sts remaining, work 1 st in Seed pattern, work one-row buttonhole over 4 sts, work next 2 sts in Seed pattern, sl 1. Work as established until Left Front matches Back length to underarm, ending with a WS row.

Shape armhole and V-neck

Next row (RS) Bind off 10 sts at beginning of row (armhole edge), work to 3 sts from start of front band, ssk, k1, 7 sts in Seed pattern, sl 1. Work 1 row even.
Decrease row (RS) K1, ssk, knit to 3 sts from front band, k2tog, k1, 7 sts in Seed pattern, sl 1. Work 1 row even. Continue working ssk at armhole edge at start of every RS row, 7 (7, 7, 9) more times, **AT SAME TIME**, continue working k2tog at front edge every RS row, 21 (25, 31, 31) more times—28 (30, 30, 32) sts. Work even until armhole measures 8 (8, 9, 10)", ending with

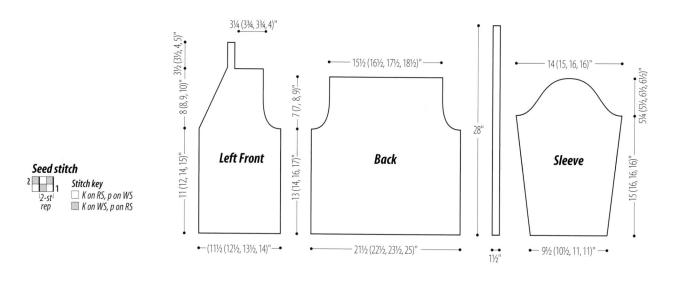

3¼ (3¾, 3¾, 4)"

8 (8, 9, 10)"   3½ (3½, 4, 4.5)"

11 (12, 14, 15)"

Left Front

←(11½ (12½, 13½, 14)→

15½ (16½, 17½, 18½)"

7 (7, 8, 9)"

13 (14, 16, 17)"

Back

←21½ (22½, 23½, 25)"→

28"

1½"

14 (15, 16, 16)"

5¼ (5½, 6½, 6½)"

Sleeve

15 (16, 16, 16)"

←9½ (10½, 11, 11)"→

a RS row. Work 8 sts for front band, place next 20 (22, 22, 24) sts on hold for shoulder. Continue 8-st band for 3½ (3½, 4, 5)" for back neck. Place all sts on hold.

RIGHT FRONT

Cast on 68 (74, 80, 84) sts. (RS) *Slip 1 purlwise with yarn in front (front edge), work in Seed pattern to 1 st remaining, k1 (side seam edge). *Next row* K1 (side seam edge), work in Seed pattern to 1 st remaining, k1 (front edge). Repeat from* for a total of 11 rows. *Next row* (WS) K1, purl to 8 sts remaining, work 7 sts in Seed pattern (front band), k1. *Next row* (RS) Sl 1, work 7 sts in Seed pattern, knit to end. Repeat last two rows until Right Front length matches Left Front to buttonhole, ending with a RS row.

Make buttonhole

Next row (WS) K1, purl to front band, work 1 st in Seed pattern, work one-row buttonhole over 4 sts, work next 2 sts in Seed pattern, sl 1. Work as established until Right Front matches Back length to underarm, ending with a RS row.

Shape armhole and V-neck

Next row (WS) Bind off 10 sts at beginning of row (armhole edge), work to 8 sts remaining, work 7 sts in Seed pattern, sl 1. *Next (Decrease) row* (RS) K1, work 7 sts in Seed pattern, k1, ssk, k to 3 sts from side edge, k2tog, k1. Work 1 row even. Continue working ssk at front edge every RS row, 21 (25, 31, 31) more times, **AT SAME TIME**, continue working k2tog at armhole edge every RS row, 7 (7, 7, 9) more times—28 (30, 30, 32) sts. Work even until armhole measures 8 (8, 9, 10)", ending with a WS row. Work 8 sts for front band, place next 20 (22, 22, 24) sts on hold for shoulder. Continue 8-st band for 3½ (3½, 4, 5)" for back neck. Place all sts on hold.

SLEEVES

Cast on 56 (62, 66, 66) stitches. (RS) Work Seed pattern for 11 rows, knitting first and last st of every row for seam edge st. *Next row* (WS) K1, purl to last st, k1. *Next row* K. Repeat last 2 rows for 1", ending with a WS row. *Next (Increase) row* (RS) K1, work lifted increase, k to last st, work lifted increase, k1—2 sts increased. Repeat Increase row every 6th row, 13 (13, 14, 14) more times—(84, 90, 96, 96) sts. Work even

until Sleeve measures 15 (16, 16, 16)", ending with a WS row.

Shape cap

Bind off 10 sts at beginning of next 2 rows. *Decrease row* (RS) K1, ssk, k to last 3 sts, k2tog, k1. Repeat Decrease row every RS row until 24 (30, 26, 26) sts remain. Bind off 3 sts at beginning of each of next 2 (4, 2, 2) rows. Bind off 18 (18, 20, 20) sts.

TIE

Cast on 9 sts. Work in Seed pattern for 28", knitting first and last st of every row. Bind off.

ASSEMBLY
Shoulders

With RS together, join Front and Back shoulder seams by binding off the 20 (22, 22, 24) sts of one shoulder in 3-needle bind-off, bind off 52 (54, 60, 62) back neck stitches; then bind off remaining 20 (22, 22, 24) sts in 3-needle bind-off.

Seams

With crochet sl st, set in sleeves, centering sleeve cap ½" forward from shoulder seam. With RS facing, join neck band sts from holders, using 3–needle bind-off. Sew neck band and back neck edge together. With crochet sl st, join sleeve and side seams. Block garment. Thread tie into the buttonholes.

5

Tremont 02

Not everyone wants to knit "fancy" stitches. This jacket is knit in stockinette stitch throughout. The shape is a bit provocative: there is a slit at the bottom of the middle back. This shorter jacket ends a few inches below the waistline. The bobble edging is crocheted after the garment is assembled and is really not difficult. A basic knowledge of single crochet, with the addition of drawing up loops in a single stitch, and a little practice will yield quick results.

Women's M: BRYSPUN
Kid-n-Ewe - 8 balls #330 Red

Tremont

Easy plus

STANDARD FIT

FINISHED measurements

Women's S (M, L)
A 41½ (45, 48½)"
B 18 (19, 22)"
C 28¼ (30, 30¼)"

10cm/4"

26 | GET GAUGE!
20

over Stockinette stitch

1 2 3 **4** 5 6

Medium weight
900 (1050, 1200) yds

4 mm/US 6
or size to obtain gauge

4 mm/US F

NOTE

1 See Techniques (page 96) for 3-needle bind-off, single crochet (sc), and chain (ch). *2* Work edge sts in Garter st (k every row). All increases and decreases are worked after the beginning edge st or before the ending edge st.

BACK

Side pieces (make 2)

Cast on 50 (54, 58) sts. K1 row (WS). Work in St st (k on RS, p on WS) until piece measures 3½" from beginning, ending with a WS row. Place all sts on hold. Make 2nd piece and leave on needle.

Joining row

Next row (RS) K 50 (54, 58) sts on needle, then k sts from hold—100 (108, 116) sts. Work until Back measures 10 (10, 12)" from beginning, end with a WS row.

Shape armhole

Next row (RS) Bind off 8 (8, 10) sts at beginning of next 2 rows. Decrease 1 st at beginning and end of every RS row 6 times—72 (80, 84) sts. Work even until armhole measures 7 (8, 9)". Place all sts on hold.

LEFT FRONT

Cast on 56 (60, 64) sts. K 1 row (WS). Work in St st until Left Front matches Back length to underarm, ending with a WS row.

Shape armhole

Next row (RS) Bind off 8 (8, 10) sts (armhole edge) at beginning of row and work to end. Work 1 row even. Decrease 1 st at beginning of every RS row 6 times—

42 (46, 48) sts. Work until Left Front measures 14 (15, 18)" from beginning, ending with a RS row.

Shape neck

Next row (WS) Bind off 10 sts (neck edge) at beginning of row, work to end. Work 1 row even. Bind off 3 sts, work to end of row. Decrease 1 st at end of every RS row 7 (9, 9) times—22 (24, 26) sts. Work even until armhole measures 8 (9, 10)". Place all sts on hold.

RIGHT FRONT

Work as for Left Front to underarm, ending with a RS row.

Shape armhole

Next row (WS) Bind off 8 (8, 10) sts (armhole edge) at beginning of row and work to end. Decrease 1 st at end of every RS row 6 times—42 (46, 48) sts. Work until Right Front measures 14 (15, 18)" from beginning, ending with a WS row.

Shape neck

Next row (RS) Bind off 10 sts (neck edge) at beginning of row, work to end. Work 1 row even. Bind off 3 sts, work to end of row. Decrease 1 st at beginning of every RS row 7 (9, 9) times—22 (24, 26) sts. Work even until armhole measures 8 (9, 10)". Place all sts on hold.

SLEEVES

Cast on 46 (52, 52) sts. K 1 row (WS). Work in St st for 1". Increase 1 st at beginning and end of next RS row. Repeat increases every 6th row 12 (12, 14)

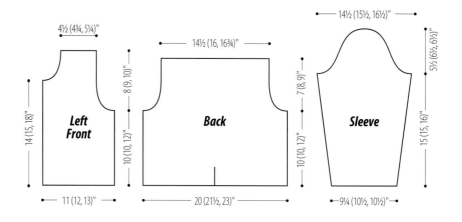

times more—72 (78, 82) sts. Work even until Sleeve measures 15 (15, 16)", ending with a WS row.

Shape cap
Bind off 8 (8, 10) sts at beginning of next 2 rows. Decrease 1 st at beginning and end of every RS row 17 (20, 20) times. Bind off 3 stitches at beginning of next 2 rows—16 sts. Bind off.

ASSEMBLY
Shoulders
With RS together, join Front and Back shoulder seams by binding off 22 (24, 26) sts of one shoulder in 3-needle bind-off; bind off 28 (32, 32) Back neck stitches; then bind off remaining 22 (24, 26) sts in 3-needle bind-off.

Front band
With RS facing, pick up and k80 (88, 102) sts along Right Front edge, 24 (28, 32) sts along Right Front neck, 26 (30, 30) sts across Back neck, 24 (28, 32) sts on Left Front neck, and 80 (88, 102) sts on Left Front edge—234 (262, 298) sts. K1 row. Bind off.

Seams
With crochet slip stitch, set in sleeves, centering sleeve cap ½" forward from the shoulder seam, then join sleeve and side seams.

EDGING
Bobble Edging
Round 1 Single crochet (sc). Join to first sc with a slip st (join), chain 1 (ch 1).
Round 2 Sc, *[(yarn around hook, draw up a loop) 3 times in the next st, draw a loop through the 7 loops on the hook] (bobble made), ch 1, skip 1 st; rep from* to end; end with 1 sc. Join, ch 1. *Note* At corners work 4 bobbles in 4 adjacent stitches (don't skip sts).
Round 3 Sc in each sc and top of each bobble. Join, fasten off.

With RS facing and using crochet hook, work Bobble edging around outside edge of jacket, starting at the right top of back vent, and ending at left side of vent with a sc. Work Bobble edging around cuffs.
Block garment.

Somerset 03

This is a quick and easy jacket for the beginner—or anyone else who enjoys a simpler knit. I chose a boucle yarn and reverse stockinette to provide fabric interest. The construction is easy: straight lines skim the body, a shawl collar is shaped by just reversing the stitch pattern and adding a few short rows, a row of single crochet finishes the edges. I designed this as a wrapped jacket and see it worn as Justine (far left) does: overlapped and fastened with a favorite belt. Nicola surprised me with another look. Oh, the versatility of knits!

Women's M: MUENCH
Relax - 8 balls #16 Oxblood

Somerset

Easy

STANDARD FIT

FINISHED measurements

Women's S (M, L, XL, XXL)
A 40½ (42½, 44½, 48½, 52½)"
B 25½ (26½, 28½, 30½, 31½)"
C 28 (28¾, 30, 32¼, 33¼)"

10cm/4"

24

16

GET GAUGE!

over Stockinette stitch

1 2 3 **4** 5 6

Medium weight
800 (900, 950, 1150) yds

4.5 mm/US 7
or size to obtain gauge

4 mm/US F

NOTES

1 See Techniques (page 96) for 3-needle bind-off, wrapping stitches on short rows, grafting, slip stitch and single crochet, and seam instructions.

BACK

Cast on 80 (84, 88, 96, 104) sts. P 1 row (WS). Work in Reverse Stockinette st (Rev St st; p on RS, k on WS) for 18 (19, 20, 21, 22)", ending with a WS row.

Shape armholes

Bind off 6 sts at beginning of next 2 rows. Decrease 1 st at beginning and end of every RS row 6 times—56 (60, 64, 72, 80) sts remain. Work even until armhole measures 7 (7, 8, 9, 9)", ending with a WS row. Place all sts on hold.

LEFT FRONT

Cast on 44 (46, 48, 52, 56) sts. P 1 row (WS). Work in Rev St st for 12 (13, 14, 15, 16)", ending with a WS row.

Begin shawl collar

Note Shawl collar will be worked in St st (k on RS, p on WS); body continues in Rev St st. *Row 1* (RS) P to the last 2 sts, k2 (2 collar sts). *Row 2* P2, k to end. *Rows 3–4* Repeat rows 1–2. *Row 5* P to 1 st before collar, k to end (1 st added to collar sts). *Rows 6, 8* P collar sts, k body sts. *Row 7* P body sts, k collar sts. Repeat rows 5–8, 15 (15, 15, 17, 19) more times—last 4 rows will be worked with 18 (18, 18, 20, 22) St st sts.

Shape armhole

AT THE SAME TIME, when Front matches Back length to underarm, ending with a WS row, bind off 6 sts at beginning of next row (armhole edge), work to end of row. Decrease 1 st at armhole edge every RS row 6 times —32 (34, 36, 40, 44) sts. Work even until armhole measures 8 (8, 9, 10, 10)", ending with a RS row. Place 14 (16, 18, 20, 22) Rev st sts on hold for shoulder.

Collar extension

Work in St st on 18 (18, 18, 20, 22) sts for 3½ (3½, 3½, 4, 4½)" ending with RS row. Work short rows as follows:
Row 1 (WS) P5, wrap next stitch and turn (see illustration).
Row 2 K5 sts.
Row 3 P5, p next st and hide wrap, p4, wrap and turn.
Row 4 K10 sts.
Row 5 P10 sts, p next st and hide wrap, p4, wrap and turn.
Row 6 K15 sts.
Row 7 P15 sts, p next st and hide wrap, p to end of row. Place all sts on hold.

RIGHT FRONT

Cast on 44 (46, 48, 52, 56) sts. P 1 row (WS). Work in Rev St st for 12 (13, 14, 15, 16)", ending with a WS row.

Shawl collar

Next row (RS) K2 for beginning of collar and work Rev St st to end of row. Continue as for Left Front, adding 1 more stitch to St st collar section every 4 rows. Last 4 rows will be worked with 18 (18, 18, 20, 22) St st sts.

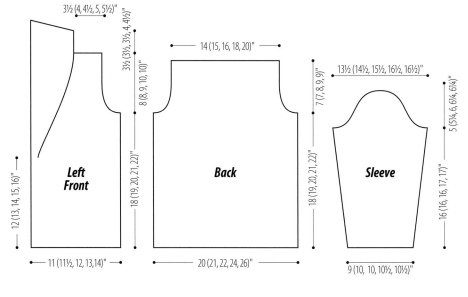

3½ (4, 4½, 5, 5½)"

3½ (3½, 3½, 4, 4½)"

8 (8, 9, 10, 10)"

14 (15, 16, 18, 20)"

13½ (14½, 15½, 16½, 16½)"

7 (7, 8, 9, 9)"

5 (5¼, 6, 6¼, 6¼)"

12 (13, 14, 15, 16)"

18 (19, 20, 21, 22)"

18 (19, 20, 21, 22)"

16 (16, 16, 17, 17)"

Left Front

Back

Sleeve

11 (11½, 12, 13, 14)"

20 (21, 22, 24, 26)"

9 (10, 10, 10½, 10½)"

Shape armhole

AT THE SAME TIME, when Front matches Back length to underarm, ending with a RS row, bind off 6 sts at beginning of next row (armhole edge). Decrease 1 st at armhole edge every RS row 6 times. Work until armhole measures 8 (8, 9, 10, 10)", ending with a WS row. Place 14 (16, 18, 20, 22) shoulder sts on hold.

Collar extension

Work in St st on 18 (18, 18, 20, 22) collar sts for 3½ (3½, 3½, 4, 4½)," ending with a WS row. Then work short rows as follows:

Row 1 (RS) K5 sts, wrap next st and turn (see illustration).
Row 2 P5 sts.
Row 3 K5 sts, k next st and hide wrap, k4, wrap and turn.
Row 4 P10 sts.
Row 5 K10 sts, k next st and hide wrap, k 4, wrap and turn.
Row 6 P15 sts.
Row 7 K15 sts, k next st and hide wrap, k to end of row. Place all sts on hold.

SLEEVES

Cast on 36 (40, 40, 42, 42) sts. P 1 row (WS). Work in Rev St st for 3 (3, 3, 2, 2½)". Increase 1 st at beginning and end of next RS row. Repeat increase every 6th row 8 (8, 10, 11, 11) more times—54 (58, 62, 66, 66 sts). Work even to 16 (16, 16, 17, 17)", ending with a WS row.

Shape cap

Bind off 6 sts at beginning of next 2 rows. Decrease 1 st at beginning and end of every RS row—12 (16, 14, 18, 18) sts. Bind off 0 (2, 0, 2, 2) sts at beginning of next two rows. Bind off 12 (12, 14, 14, 14) sts.

ASSEMBLY

Shoulders

With RS together, join Front and Back shoulder seams by binding off the 14 (16, 18, 20, 22) sts of one shoulder in 3-needle bind-off; bind off 28 (28, 28, 32, 36) back neck stitches; then bind off remaining 14 (16, 18, 20, 22) sts in 3-needle bind-off.

Collar

Graft the collar ends together and sew collar extension to back neck.

Seams

With crochet slip st, set in sleeves, centering sleeve cap ½" forward from the shoulder seam, then join sleeve and side seams.

Edging

Work one row of single crochet around all edges of jacket body and sleeves. Block garment.

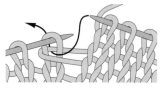

WRAPPING STS ON SHORT ROWS

Each short row adds two rows of knitting across a section of the work. Since the work is turned before completing a row, stitches must be wrapped at the turn to prevent holes.

KNIT SIDE

Wrap and turn With yarn in front, slip next stitch as if to purl. Bring yarn to back of work and slip stitch back to left needle as shown. Turn work.

Hide wrap When you come to the wrap on the following knit row, make it less visible on the purl side by knitting the wrap together with the stitch it wraps.

PURL SIDE

Wrap and turn With yarn in back, slip next stitch as if to purl. Bring yarn to front of work and slip stitch back to left needle as shown. Turn work.

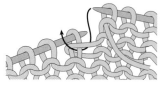

Hide wrap When you come to the wrap on the following purl row, make it less visible by inserting right needle under wrap as shown, placing the wrap on the left needle, and purling it together with the stitch it wraps.

Chardon 04

Left, Women's M: WOOL IN THE WOODS
Pizazz - 5 skeins Mica

This style of jacket became popular when Nehru ruled India after World War II. It is as popular today as when it was first introduced. The jacket's lines lend themselves to simple knitting. The garment is slightly fitted and has a narrow stand-up collar. I used reverse stockinette stitch to display the beauty of a textured yarn.

Chardon

STANDARD FIT

FINISHED measurements

Women's S (M, L)
A 41½ (44, 46)"
B 22½ (24½, 25½)"
C 27¾ (29½, 30¾)"

10cm/4"

18 **GET GAUGE!**

12

over Reverse stockinette stitch

1 2 3 4 **5** 6

Bulky weight
850 (1000, 1100) yds

Seven (eight, eight) ¾" buttons

6 mm/US 10
or size to obtain gauge

4 mm/US F

NOTES

1 See Techniques (page 96) for 3-needle bind-off, ssk, lifted increase, one-row buttonhole, crab stitch crochet, and seam instructions.

BACK

Cast on 60 (64, 68) sts. P 1 row (WS). Work even in Reverse Stockinette st (Rev St st; p on RS, k on WS) for 5 rows. *Next row* (WS) K13 (14, 15), k2tog, place marker (pm), ssk, k26 (28, 30), k2tog, pm, ssk, k13 (14, 15). Repeat decreases every 4th row 4 more times, working k2tog before markers and ssk after markers—40 (44, 48) sts. Work 2 (3, 3)" even, slipping markers every row and ending with a RS row. *Next row* (WS) *K to 1 st before marker, work lifted increase in st before and after marker; repeat from* once more, k to end of row. Repeat increase row every 4th row 4 more times—60 (64, 68) sts. Work even until Back measures 15 (17, 17)", ending with a WS row.

Shape armholes

Bind off 6 sts at beginning of next 2 rows. Decrease 1 st at beginning and end of each WS row 4 times—40 (44, 48) sts. Work even until armhole measures 7 (7, 8)", ending with a WS row. Place sts on hold.

LEFT FRONT

Cast on 34 (36, 38) sts. P 1 row (WS). Work 5 rows in Rev St st.

Shape waist

Next row (WS) K18 (19, 20), k2tog, pm, ssk, k12 (13, 14). Repeat decreases each side of marker every 4th row 4 more times—24 (26, 28) sts. Work 2 (3, 3)" even, ending with a RS row. *Next row* (WS) K to 1 st before marker, work lifted increase in st before and after marker, k to end of row. Repeat increase row every 4th row 4 more times—34 (36, 38) sts. Work even until Left Front matches Back length to armhole shaping, ending with a WS row.

Shape armhole

Next row (RS) Bind off 6 sts (armhole edge), work to end of row. Work 1 row even. Decrease 1 st at armhole edge every WS row 4 times—24 (26, 28) sts. Work even until Left Front measures 20 (21, 22)", ending with a RS row.

Shape neck

Next row (WS) Bind off 7 (8, 9) sts (neck edge). Decrease 1 st at neck edge every WS row 4 times—13 (14, 15) sts. Work even until armhole measures 8 (8, 9)", ending with a WS row. Place sts on hold.

Mark for buttons

Mark placement of 7 (8, 8) buttons along center front edge, with the top of one button ½" from top edge, the bottom of one button 1½" from bottom, and the others spaced evenly between.

RIGHT FRONT

Work as for Left Front to Shape waist.

Shape waist and make buttonholes

Next row (WS) K12 (13, 14), ssk, pm, k2tog, k18 (19, 20). Repeat decreases each side of marker every 4th row 4

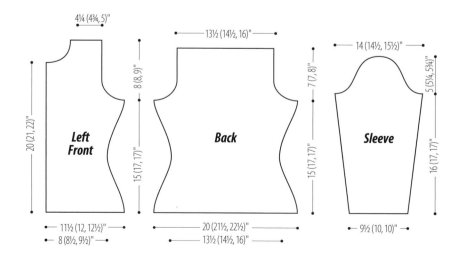

4¼ (4¾, 5)"

13½ (14½, 16)"

14 (14½, 15½)"

8 (8, 9)"

7 (7, 8)"

5 (5¼, 5¾)"

20 (21, 22)"

15 (17, 17)"

15 (17, 17)"

16 (17, 17)"

Left Front

Back

Sleeve

11½ (12, 12½)"

8 (8½, 9½)"

20 (21½, 22½)"

13½ (14½, 16)"

9½ (10, 10)"

more times—24 (26, 28) sts. Work 2 (3, 3)" even, ending with a RS row. **Next row** (WS) K to 1 st before marker, work lifted increase in st before and after marker, k to end of row. Repeat increase row every 4th row 4 more times—34 (36, 38) sts. Work even until Right Front matches Back length to underarm, ending with a RS row. **AT SAME TIME,** using Left Front as a guide for placement of buttonholes, *on WS row at center of button, k to 7 sts remaining, work one-row buttonhole over 4 sts, work to end. Repeat from* for remaining buttonholes.

Shape armhole

Next row (WS) Bind off 6 sts (armhole edge), work to end of row. Decrease 1 st at armhole edge on every WS row 4 times—24 (26, 28) sts. Work even until Right Front measures 20 (21, 22)", ending with a WS row.

Shape neck

Next row (RS) Bind off 7 (8, 9) sts (neck edge), work to end of row. Work 1 row even. Decrease 1 st at neck edge every WS row 4 times—13 (14, 15) sts. Work even until armhole measures 8 (8, 9)", ending with a WS row. Place sts on hold.

SLEEVES

Cast on 28 (30, 30) sts. P1 row (WS). Work 5 rows in Rev St st. Increase 1 st at beginning and end of next (WS) row. Repeat increases on WS rows every 2" 6 (6, 7) more times—42 (44, 46) sts. Work even until Sleeve measures 16 (17, 17)", ending with a WS row.

Shape cap

Bind off 6 sts at beginning of next 2 rows. Decrease 1 st at beginning and end of every RS row until 8 sts remain. Bind off.

ASSEMBLY

Shoulders

With RS together, join Front and Back shoulder seams by binding off the 13 (14, 15) sts of one shoulder in 3-needle bind-off; bind off 14 (16, 18) Back neck stitches; then bind off remaining 13 (14, 15) sts in 3-needle bind-off.

Collar

With WS facing, pick up and k14 (14, 16) for Right side neck, 14 (16, 18) sts for Back neck, and 14 (14, 16) for the Left side neck—42 (44, 50) sts. P next (RS) row and continue in Rev St st for 3". Bind off. Fold in half and sew in place on inside.

Seams

With crochet slip stitch, set in sleeves, centering sleeve cap ½" forward from the shoulder seam, then join sleeve and side seams.

Edging

Work 1 row of crab st crochet around cuff and all edges of jacket. Block garment.

Fairfield 05

Women's L: PLYMOUTH
Galway - 7 balls Cream

This jacket was inspired by a favorite vase of mine, made by the Irish company Belleek Pottery. The creamy translucent china appears to be woven like a basket, is topped by a scalloped edging, and is perfect for reproducing in a knit. This knit-and-purl basket weave pattern makes a beautiful fabric for a straight jacket. A lace pattern provides the scallops that edge the shawl collar.

Fairfield

NOTES

1 See Techniques (page 96) for 3-needle bind-off, long-tail cast-on, loop cast-on, ssk, buttonhole placement, and seam instructions. *2* Use long-tail cast-on except for buttonholes. *3* Work edge sts in Garter st (k every row). All increases and decreases are worked after the beginning edge st or before the ending edge st. *4* Slip all sts purlwise.

Basket Weave pattern (multiple of 8 plus 2 sts; includes edge sts)
Row 1 (WS) K1, p across, end k1.
Row 2 K1, p2, k2, *p6, k2; repeat from*, end p2, k1.
Row 3 K5, *p2, k6; repeat from*, end last repeat k3.
Row 4 Repeat Row 2.
Row 5 Repeat Row 1.
Row 6 K1, *p6, k2 ; repeat from*, end k1.
Row 7 K1, *p2, k6; repeat from*, end k7.
Row 8 Repeat Row 6.

BACK

Cast on 98 (114, 122, 130) sts. Work in Basket Weave pattern until Back measures 13 (14, 15, 16)", ending with a WS row.

Shape armholes

Bind off 7 (11, 11, 13) sts at beginning of next 2 rows. Decrease 1 st at beginning and end of every RS row 6 (8, 10, 10) times—72 (76, 80, 84) sts. Work even until armhole measures approximately 7 (7, 8, 8)", ending with pattern row 4 or 8. Place all sts on hold.

POCKET LININGS (make 2)

Cast on 24 sts. Work in St st (k on RS, p on WS) for 4". Place all sts on hold.

LEFT FRONT

Cast on 50 (58, 66, 74) sts. Work in Basket Weave Pattern **EXCEPT** at end of every RS row, work to 1 st, and slip 1 with yarn in front (sl1 wyif). Continue sl1 wyif until start of neck shaping. Work until Left Front measures 4½", ending with row 4 or 8.

Place pocket

Next row (WS) Work 12 (16, 20, 24) sts, bind off 24 sts, work 13 (17, 21, 25) sts. *Next row* Work 13 (17, 21, 25) sts, with RS of pocket facing, work 24 sts from hold, work to end of row. Work until Left Front matches Back length to underarm, ending with a WS row.

Shape armhole and neck

Bind off 7 (11, 11, 13) sts (armhole edge), work to 3 sts remaining, k2tog (neck edge), k1. Work 1 row even. Decrease 1 st at armhole edge every RS row 7 (9, 11, 11) times, **AT SAME TIME**, at neck edge, decrease 1 st every RS row 0 (0, 2, 6) more times, then every 4th row 13 (13, 15, 15) times—22 (24, 26, 28) sts. Work even until armhole measures 8 (8, 9, 9)", ending with row 4 or 8. Place all sts on hold.

RIGHT FRONT

Work as for Left Front to Place pocket **EXCEPT** at the end of every WS row, sl1 wyif until start of neck shaping.

Place pocket

Next row (WS) Work 13 (17, 21, 25) sts, bind off 24 sts, work 13 (17, 21, 25) sts. *Next row* Work 12 (16, 20, 24) sts; with RS of pocket facing, work 24 sts from hold; work to end of row. Work until Right Front matches Back length to underarm, ending with a RS row.

Shape armhole and neck

Bind off 7 (11, 11, 13) sts (armhole edge), work to end of row. *Next row* (RS) K1, ssk (neck edge), work to 2 sts remaining, decrease 1 st at armhole edge. Decrease 1 st at armhole edge every RS row 6 (8, 10, 10) more times, **AT SAME TIME,** decrease 1 st at neck edge every RS row 0 (0, 2, 6) more times, then every 4th row 13 (13, 15, 15) times—22 (24, 26, 28) sts. Work even until armhole measures 8 (8, 9, 9)", ending with row 4 or 8. Place all sts on hold.

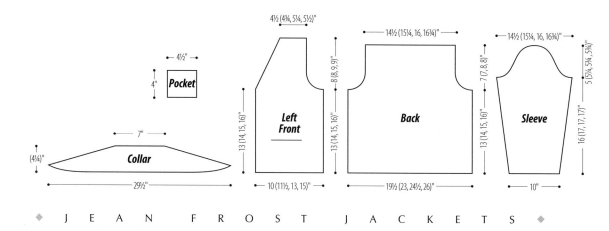

SLEEVES

Cast on 50 (50, 50, 50) sts. Work in Basket Weave pattern for 2", ending with a WS row. Continue in pattern, increasing 1 st at beginning and end of row (working increases into pattern) on next row, then every 8 (8, 6, 6)th row, 10 (12, 14, 16) more times—(70, 76, 80, 84) sts. Work even until sleeve measures 16 (17, 17, 17)", ending with a WS row.

Shape cap

Bind off 7 (11, 11, 13) sts at beginning of next 2 rows. Decrease 1 st at beginning and end of every RS row until 18 (12, 12, 12) sts remain. Bind off.

COLLAR

Cast on 147 sts.

Row 1 (WS) K1, p to last st, k1.

Row 2 K1, k across, wrapping yarn over needle twice for each st, end k1.

Row 3 K1, slip 4, dropping extra wraps from previous row, then sl 4 back to left-hand needle and k4tog, *yo, (k1, yo) 5 times, slip 7, dropping extra wraps, then slip 7 back to left-hand needle and k7tog; repeat from*, end last repeat slip 4, dropping extra wraps, then slip 4 back to left-hand needle and k4tog, k1.

Row 4 K to 3 sts, k2tog, k1—146 sts.

Row 5 K.

Row 6 K.

Change to Basket Weave pattern, work Rows 5–7, maintaining garter st edges and starting as shown on chart. *Next row* (RS) At beginning of next two rows, bind off 8 sts. Work 2 rows even. Repeat last 3 rows 7 more times—34 sts. Bind off.

ASSEMBLY

Shoulders

With RS together, join Front and Back shoulder seams by binding off the 22 (24, 26, 28) sts of one shoulder in 3-needle bind-off; bind off 28 back neck stitches; then bind off remaining 22 (24, 26, 28) sts in 3-needle bind-off.

Seams

Center collar at back of neck with ends at beginning of V-neck shaping; overcast edges together. With crochet slip st, set in sleeves, centering sleeve cap ½" forward from the shoulder seam. Sew pocket linings in place. With crochet slip st, join sleeve and side seams.

Mark for buttons

Mark Left Front for placement of 3 (3, 3, 4) buttons, the top of one button just below the start of V-neck shaping, the bottom of one button about 4" from bottom edge, and the others placed evenly between.

Left Front edging

With RS facing, starting at lower edge, work chain st between the slipped st and the first st of pattern, ending at the first V-neck decrease.

Right Front edging

Work as for Left Front, **EXCEPT** when you reach marker for a buttonhole, chain over an edge stitch, chain 3 and skip a stitch, chain over an edge stitch, chain to next buttonhole (see illustration). Block garment. Sew on buttons.

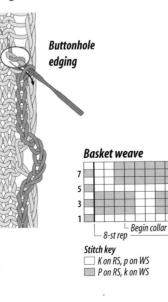

Buttonhole edging

Basket weave

```
7          8
           6
5
           4
3
           2
1
   8-st rep    Begin collar
```

Stitch key

☐ K on RS, p on WS
▩ P on RS, k on WS

Trilling 06

The jackets in this book reflect the great influence that Coco Chanel has had on my designs. The Trilling jacket was inspired by a design by Karl Lagerfeld, who ruled the House of Chanel after Coco's death. With a bolero shape that just skims the waist, the jacket is embellished by four pockets and buttons on the cuffs. The knitted fabric has a woven appearance, yet a supple drape. Together, these features epitomize the softly tailored style of the Chanel jacket.

Women's M: DALE OF NORWAY
Heilo - 12 balls # 9335

Trilling

Intermediate

STANDARD FIT

FINISHED measurements

Women's S (M, L)
A 39½ (43, 47)"
B 18½ (19½, 21½)"
C 27¾ (29¼, 30¾)"

10cm/4"

36 | 24

over Basket weave pattern

1 2 **3** 4 5 6

Light weight
1400 (1600, 1800) yds

Four ¾" buttons

3.75 mm/US 5
or size to obtain gauge

4 mm/US F

NOTES

1 See Techniques (page 96) for 3-needle bind-off, crab stitch, and seam instructions. **2** Work edge sts in Garter st (k every row). All increases and decreases are worked after the beginning edge st or before the ending edge st. **3** Slip all sts purlwise.

Basket weave (multiple of 4 sts; includes edge sts)
Row 1 (RS) K1, *k2, p2; repeat from*, end k1.
Row 2 K1, *k2, p2; repeat from*, end k1.
Row 3 K1, *k2, slip 2 purlwise with yarn in front (sl2 wyif); repeat from*, end k1.
Row 4 K1, *slip 2 purlwise with yarn in back (sl2 wyib)p2; repeat from*, end k1.
Row 5 Repeat row 2.
Row 6 Repeat row 1.
Row 7 K1, *sl2 wyif, k2; repeat from*, end k1.
Row 8 K1, *p2, sl2 wyib; repeat from*, end k1.

BACK

Cast on 114 (122, 130) sts. P 1 row (WS). Work in Basket weave pattern for 11 (11, 12)", ending with a WS row.
Shape armhole
Bind off 9 (10, 11) sts at beginning of next 2 rows. Decrease 1 st at beginning and end of every RS row 8(9, 10) times—80 (84, 88) sts. Work even until armhole measures approximately 7 (8, 9)", ending with row 4 or 8. Place sts on hold.

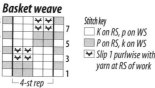

Basket weave

Stitch key
☐ K on RS, p on WS
▨ P on RS, k on WS
⩔ Slip 1 purlwise with yarn at RS of work

└─ 4-st rep ─┘

LEFT FRONT

Cast on 62 (70, 78) sts. P 1 row (WS). Work in Basket weave pattern until Left Front matches Back length to underarm, ending with a WS row.
Shape armhole
Next row (RS) Bind off 9 (10, 11) sts at beginning of next row, work to end of row. Decrease 1 st at armhole edge every RS row 9 (10, 11) times—44 (50, 56) sts. Work even until Left Front measures 15 (16, 17)", ending with row 3 or 7.
Shape neck
Next row (WS) Bind off 10 (10, 12) sts (neck edge), work to end of row. Work 1 row even. **Next row** Bind off 4 sts, work to end of row. Decrease 1 st at neck edge every RS row 4 (8, 10) times—26 (28, 30) sts. Work even until armhole measures approximately 8 (9, 10)", ending with row 4 or 8. Place sts on hold.

RIGHT FRONT

Work as for Left Front to underarm, ending with a RS row.
Shape armhole
Next row (WS) Bind off 9 (10, 11) sts at the beginning of next row, work to end of row. Decrease 1 st at armhole edge every RS row 9 (10, 11) times—44 (50, 56) sts. Work until Right Front measures 15 (16, 17)", ending with row 4 or 8.
Shape neck
Next row (RS) Bind off 10 (10, 12) sts (neck edge), work to end of row. Work 1 row even. **Next row** Bind off 4 sts, work to end of row. Decrease 1 st at neck edge every RS row 4 (8, 10) times—26 (28, 30) sts.

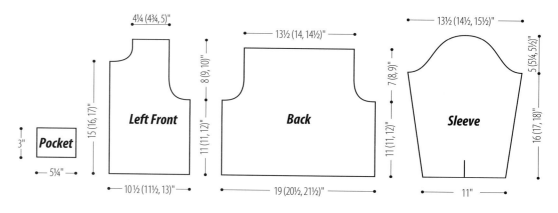

4¼ (4¾, 5)"
13½ (14, 14½)"
13½ (14½, 15½)"

Pocket
3"
5¼"

Left Front
15 (16, 17)"
8 (9, 10)"
11 (11, 12)"
10½ (11½, 13)"

Back
7 (8, 9)"
11 (11, 12)"
19 (20½, 21½)"

Sleeve
5 (5¼, 5½)"
16 (17, 18)"
11"

Work even until armhole measures approximately 8 (9, 10)", ending with row 1 or 5. Place sts on hold.

POCKETS (Make 4)
Cast on 32 sts. (WS) Purl 1 row. Work in Basket weave pattern for 3", ending with row 4 or 8. Bind off. Crochet 1 row of crab st across top of each pocket.

SLEEVES
Cuff (Make 2)
Cast on 34 sts. P 1 row (WS). Work in Basket weave pattern for 3 repeats (24 rows). Place sts on hold. Repeat from *to* **EXCEPT** leave sts on needle.
Next row (RS) Work row 1 of Basket weave pattern across 32 sts of cuff (2 sts remaining), p2tog, continue in pattern on sts from hold, beginning first repeat k2tog, k1—66 sts. Work even in pattern, increasing 1 st at beginning and end of next RS row, and every 8th row 6 (9, 12) more times—80 (86, 92) sts. Work even in pattern until sleeve measures 16 (17, 18)", ending with a WS row.
Shape cap
Next row (RS) Bind off 9 (10, 11) sts at beginning of next 2 rows. Decrease 1 st each end of every RS row until 16 (18, 20) sts remain. Bind off.

ASSEMBLY
Pockets
Place lower pockets 2½" above bottom edge and 2" from front edge. Place upper pockets ½" below armhole bind-off and 2" from front edge. Sew in place.
Shoulders
With RS together, join Front and Back shoulder seams by binding off 26 (28, 30) sts of one shoulder in 3-needle bind-off; bind off 28 (28, 28) back neck sts; then bind off remaining 26 (28, 30) sts in 3-needle bind-off.
Seams
With crochet slip st, set in sleeves, centering sleeve cap ½" forward from the shoulder seam, then join sleeve and side seams.
Edging
Crochet a single row of crab st around edges of body and sleeve cuffs. Sew front cuff over back cuff along edge. Sew buttons on front cuffs. Block garment.

Copley 07

An all-over nubby fabric enhances the simple lines of this V-neck jacket. Pockets and picot-edged hems, worked on a background of easy-to-knit Rice stitch, are smart accents.

Women's M

Copley

STANDARD FIT

FINISHED measurements

Women's S (M, L, XL)
A 40 (42½, 47½, 50½)"
B 18½ (19½, 21½, 24½)"
C 28¾ (30, 31, 32½)"

10cm/4"

28 GET GAUGE!

20

over Rice pattern

1 2 3 **4** 5 6

Medium weight

1200 (1350, 1500, 1700) yds

Four ¾" buttons

4 mm/US 6
or size to obtain gauge

4 mm/US F

NOTES

1 See Techniques (page 96) for 3-needle bind-off, k in back of st, one-row buttonhole, and seam instructions. *2* Work edge sts in Garter st (k every row). All increases and decreases are worked after the beginning edge st or before the ending edge st.

Rice pattern (multiple of 2 sts plus 1; includes edge sts)
Row 1 (WS) K.
Row 2 K1, *p1, k1 in back of st; repeat from*, end p1, k1.

Picot edge

P 1 row, k 1 row, p 1 row. *Next row* (fold line) *K2tog, yo; repeat from*, end k1. Work in St st for 4 rows.

BACK

Cast on 103 (109, 121, 131) sts. Work Picot edge. *Next row* (WS) Work in Rice pattern until Back measures 11 (12, 13, 15)" from fold line, ending with a WS row.

Shape armholes

Bind off 8 (8, 10, 10) sts at beginning of next 2 rows. Decrease 1 st at beginning and end of every RS row 6 (6, 8, 10) times—75 (81, 85, 91) sts. Work even until armhole measures 7 (7, 8, 9)", ending with a RS row. Place all sts on hold.

POCKET LININGS (Make 2)

Cast on 24 sts. Work in St st (k 1 row, p 1 row) for 3". Place all sts on hold.

LEFT FRONT

Cast on 49 (53, 59, 63) sts. Work Picot edge. *Next row* (WS) Work Rice pattern for 4", ending with a WS row.

Place pocket

Next row (RS) Work 12 (14, 17, 19) sts, work next 24 sts and place on hold for pocket opening, work to end of row. *Next row* Work 13 (15, 18, 20) sts, work in pattern across WS of 24 sts of pocket, work to end of row. Work until Left Front matches Back length to underarm, ending with a WS row.

Shape armhole and V-neck

Bind off 8 (8, 10, 10) sts at beginning of row (armhole edge), work to 3 sts remaining and ssk, k1 (neck edge). Work 1 row even. Decrease 1 st at armhole edge every RS row 6 (6, 8, 10) times. **AT SAME TIME**, decrease 1 st at neck edge every 4th row 10 (11, 13, 14) more times—24 (27, 27, 28) sts. Work even until armhole measures 8 (8, 9, 10)", ending with a WS row. Place all sts on hold.

RIGHT FRONT

Work as for Left Front to Place pocket, ending with a WS row.

Place pocket

Next row (RS) Work 13 (15, 18, 20) sts, work next 24 sts and place on hold for pocket opening, work to end of row. *Next row* Work 12 (14, 17, 19) sts, work in pattern across WS of 24 sts of pocket, work to end of row. Work until Right Front matches Back length to underarm, ending with a RS row.

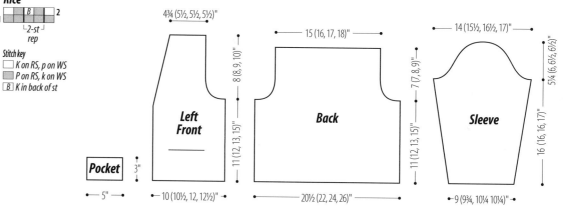

Rice

B

1 — 2

2-st rep

Stitch key
☐ K on RS, p on WS
▨ P on RS, k on WS
B K in back of st

Pocket — 3"

Left Front

4¾ (5½, 5½, 5½)"

8 (8, 9, 10)"

11 (12, 13, 15)"

— 5" —

— 10 (10½, 12, 12½)" —

Back

15 (16, 17, 18)"

7 (7, 8, 9)"

11 (12, 13, 15)"

— 20½ (22, 24, 26)" —

Sleeve

14 (15½, 16½, 17)"

5¼ (6, 6½, 6½)"

16 (16, 16, 17)"

— 9 (9¾, 10¼ 10¼)" —

Shape armhole and V-neck

Bind off 8 (8, 10, 10) sts at beginning of row (armhole edge), work to end of row. *Next row* (RS) K1, k2tog, (neck edge) work to 2 sts remaining and decrease 1 (armhole edge). Work 1 row even. Decrease 1 st at armhole edge every RS row 5 (5, 7, 9) more times. **AT SAME TIME,** decrease 1 st at neck edge every 4th row 10 (11, 13, 14) more times—24 (27, 27, 28) sts. Work even until armhole measures 8 (8, 9, 10)", ending with a WS row. Place all sts on hold.

SLEEVES

Cast on 45 (49, 51, 51) sts. Work Picot edge. Then work Rice pattern for 1", ending with a WS row. Increase 1 st at beginning and end of next row. Repeat increase every 1 (1, ¾ ¾)" 12 (13, 15, 16) more times—71 (77, 83, 85) sts. Work even to 16 (16, 16, 17)" from fold line, ending with a WS row.

Shape cap

Bind off 8 (8, 10, 10) sts at beginning of next two rows. Decrease 1 st at beginning and end of every RS row until 19 (19, 17, 19) sts remain. Bind off.

ASSEMBLY

Pocket trim

Work Picot edge on sts from hold. Fold edging at fold line and sew on inside. Sew pocket linings in place and sew ends of trim down.

Shoulders

With RS together, join Front and Back shoulder seams by binding off the 24 (27, 27, 28) sts of one shoulder in 3-needle bind-off; bind off 27 (27, 31, 35) back neck stitches; then bind off remaining 24 (27, 27, 28) sts in 3-needle bind-off.

Mark for buttons

Mark Left Front for 4 buttons, with the top of the top button about ½" down from the start of the V-neck shaping, and 2" between each of the remaining buttons.
Mark Right Front for 4 matching buttonholes.

Front and neck border

With RS facing, starting at fold line of Right Front side, pick up and k approximately 100 (106, 112, 120) sts along Right Front, 27 (27, 31, 35) sts along back neck, and 100 (106, 112, 120) sts along Left Front—227 (239, 255, 275) sts. Work Picot edge **EXCEPT** on 2nd and 6th rows, k to marker for first buttonhole and work one-row buttonhole over 3 sts; repeat at each marker, with same number of sts between each buttonhole, and work to end of row. Complete Picot edge and bind off. Fold edging to inside and sew down. Overcast two layers of buttonhole together. Sew on buttons.

Seams

With crochet slip st, set in sleeves, centering sleeve cap ½" forward from the shoulder seam; then join sleeve and side seams. Block garment.

Piedmont 08

The beauty of a classic yarn shines in this understated jacket. Elegant, smooth lines and no-fuss finishing put the focus on a simply beautiful fabric.

Women's M: BRYSPUN
Kid-n-Ewe - MC 8 balls #120 Gray, CC 7 balls #110 Black

Piedmont

STANDARD FIT

FINISHED measurements

Women's S (M, L)
A 39 (44, 47½)"
B 21½ (23½, 25½)"
C 28 (29½, 30¼)"

10cm/4"

48 **GET GAUGE!** 28

over Dot pattern

1 2 3 **4** 5 6

Medium weight
Main color (MC)
900 (1000, 1100) yds
Contrasting color (CC)
800 (900, 1000) yds

Six ¾" buttons

4 mm/US 6
or size to obtain gauge

4 mm/US F

NOTES

1 See Techniques (page 96) for ssk, 3-needle bind-off, single crochet, crab st crochet, and seam instructions. *2* Work edge sts in Garter st (k every row). All increases and decreases are done after the beginning edge st or before the ending edge st. *3* Carry contrasting color not in use loosely up edge. *4* Slip all sts purlwise.

Dot pattern

(Multiple of 4 sts plus 2; includes edge sts)
Row 1 (RS) With CC, k1, *slip 2 purlwise with yarn in back (sl2 wyib), k2; repeat from*, k1.
Row 2 With CC, k1, *slip 2 purlwise with yarn in front (sl2 wyif), k2; repeat from*, k1.
Rows 3–4 Repeat rows 1–2.
Row 5 With MC, k.
Row 6 With MC, k1, p to last st, k1.
Row 7 With CC, k1, *k2, sl2 wyib; repeat from*, end k1.
Row 8 With CC, k1, *k2, sl2 wyif; repeat from*, end k1.
Rows 9–10 Repeat rows 7–8.
Row 11 With MC, k.
Row 12 With MC, k1, p to last st, k1.

BACK

With MC, cast on 138 (154, 166) sts. P1 row (WS). Work even in Dot pattern until Back measures 14 (15, 16)", ending with a WS row.
Shape armholes
Bind off 10 sts at beginning of next 2 rows. Decrease 1 st at beginning and end of every RS row 7 (10, 10)

times—(104, 114, 126) sts. Work even until armhole measures approximately 7 (8, 9)", ending with row 5 or 11. Place all sts on hold.

LEFT FRONT

With MC, cast on 74 (82, 90) sts. P1 row (WS). Work in Dot pattern until Left Front matches Back length to underarm, ending with a WS row.
Shape armhole
Next row (RS) Bind off 10 sts at beginning of row (armhole edge), work to end. Work 1 row even. Decrease 1 st at armhole edge every RS row 7 (10, 10) times—57 (62, 70) sts. Work even until Left Front measures approximately 18 (20, 22)", ending with row 4 or 10.
Shape neck
Next row (WS) Bind off 10 (10, 14) sts (neck edge), work to end of row. Work 1 row even. *Next row* Bind off 3 sts, work to end of row. Work ssk at neck edge every RS row 10 (11, 11) times—34 (38, 42) sts. Work even until armhole measures approximately 8 (9, 10)", ending with row 4 or 10. Place all sts on hold.

RIGHT FRONT

Work same as Left Front to underarm, ending with a RS row.
Shape armhole
Next row (WS) Bind off 10 sts at beginning of row (armhole edge), work to end of row. Decrease 1 st at armhole edge every RS row 7 (10, 10) times—57 (62, 70) sts. Work even until Right Front measures 18 (20, 22)", ending with row 5 or 11.

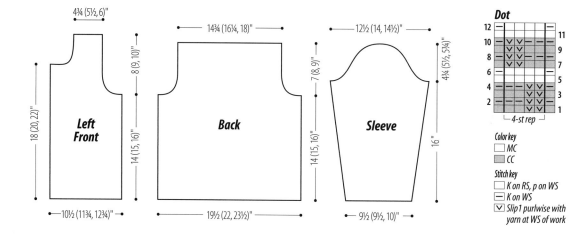

4¾ (5½, 6)"

8 (9, 10)"

14¾ (16¼, 18)"

12½ (14, 14½)"

4¾ (5½, 5¾)"

18 (20, 22)"

14 (15, 16)"

14 (15, 16)"

16"

7 (8, 9)"

Left Front

Back

Sleeve

10½ (11¾, 12¾)"

19½ (22, 23½)"

9½ (9½, 10)"

Dot

⌞4-st rep⌟

Color key
☐ MC
▨ CC

Stitch key
☐ K on RS, p on WS
— K on WS
☑ Slip1 purlwise with yarn at WS of work

Shape neck
Next row (RS) Bind off 10 (10, 14) sts (neck edge), work to end of row. Work 1 row even. *Next row* Bind off 3 sts, work to end of row. K2tog at neck edge every RS row 10 (11, 11) times—34 (38, 42) sts. Work even until armhole measures approximately 8 (9, 10)", ending with row 4 or 10. Place all sts on hold.

SLEEVES
With MC, cast on 66 (66, 70) sts. P 1 row (WS). Work in Dot pattern for 1", ending with a WS row. Increase 1 st at beginning and end of next (RS) row. Repeat increases on RS row every 1 (¾ ¾)", 10 (15, 15) more times—88 (98, 102) sts. Work even until Sleeve measures approximately 16", ending with a WS row.

Shape cap
Bind off 10 sts at beginning of next 2 rows. Decrease 1 st at beginning and end of every RS row 28 (33, 35) times—12 sts. Work 1 row even. Bind off.

ASSEMBLY
Shoulders
With RS together and using MC, join Front and Back shoulder seams by binding off the 34 (38, 42) sts of one shoulder in 3-needle bind-off; bind off 36 (38, 42) Back neck stitches; then bind off remaining 34 (38, 42) sts in 3-needle bind-off.

Seams
With MC and crochet slip st, set in sleeves, centering sleeve cap ½" forward from shoulder seam; then join sleeve and side seams.

Mark for buttonholes
Mark Left Front for placement of 6 buttons, the top of one button ½" below top edge, the bottom of one button about 2" from bottom edge, the others spaced evenly between. Sew on buttons. Mark Right Front for matching buttonholes.

Crochet edging and buttonholes
With RS facing and starting at bottom of Right side seam with MC, work 1 round of single crochet (sc) around all edges. Join with slip st, chain (ch) 1. Sc 2nd round, **EXCEPT** when you reach buttonhole markers, ch 3 and skip 3 sts, work sc in 4th st. Do not join; ch1. Work one row of crab st, working 3 sts in each of the ch-3 buttonholes. Repeat edging around sleeve cuffs. Block garment.

Claridge 09

Women's M: PLYMOUTH
Galway - MC 6 balls #109 Taupe, CC 3 balls #114 Pink

I believe the Chanel style is based on the Janker jacket worn by the people who live in the alpine regions of Europe. This practical garment is made of fulled fabric that is windproof and very warm. Coco Chanel spent some time in Switzerland during World War II where she must have seen this type of jacket. When she returned to designing after the war, Chanel produced the timeless garment we now refer to as a Chanel jacket. I gave this jacket four pockets, and slits at the bottom of each sleeve. It is finished with single crochet braid and a picot edging. Crocheted buttons are sewn on with the contrasting-color yarn.

Claridge

Intermediate

STANDARD FIT

FINISHED measurements

Women's S (M, L)
A 40 (43½, 47)"
B 24 (24½, 27½)"
C 28 (30¼, 31¼)"

10cm/4"

48 | GET GAUGE!
24

over Garter slip pattern

1 2 3 **4** 5 6

Medium weight
Main color (MC)
1200 (1400, 1600) yds
Contrasting color (CC)
800 (900, 1000) yds

Seventeen ½" plastic rings

3.75 mm/US 5
or size to obtain gauge

4 mm/US F

NOTES

1 See Techniques (page 96) for 3-needle bind-off, buttonhole placement, crochet directions, and seam instructions. **2** Work edge sts in Garter st (k every row). All increases and decreases are worked after the beginning edge st or before the ending edge st. **3** Carry yarn not in use loosely up edge. **4** Slip all sts purlwise.

Garter slip pattern (Multiple of 2 sts plus 1; includes edge sts)
Row 1, 2 With MC, k.
Row 3 (RS) With CC, k2, *slip 1 st purlwise with yarn in back (sl 1 wyib), k1; repeat from*, end k2.
Row 4 With CC, k2, *slip 1 st purlwise with yarn in front (sl 1 wyif), k1; repeat from*, end k2.
Row 5, 6 With MC, k.
Row 7 With CC, k1, *sl 1 wyib, k1; repeat from*, end k2.
Row 8 With CC, k1, *sl 1 wyif, k1; repeat from*, end k2.

BACK

With MC, cast on 123 (135, 145) sts. P 1 row (WS). Work in Garter slip pattern until Back measures approximately 13 (13, 15)", ending with a WS row.

Shape armholes

Bind off 10 sts at beginning of next 2 rows. Decrease 1 st at beginning and end of every RS row 10 times—83 (95, 105) sts. Work even in pattern until armhole measures approximately 7 (8, 8)", ending with pattern row 1 or 5. Place all sts on hold.

POCKET LININGS (Make 4)

With CC, cast on 32 sts. Work in St st (k 1 row, p 1 row) for 3½". Place all sts on hold.

LEFT FRONT

With MC, cast on 63 (67, 73) sts. P 1 row (WS). Work in Garter slip pattern for approximately 4", ending with row 8.

Place lower pocket

Work 16 (18, 21) sts, bind off 32 sts for pocket opening, work to end of row. **Next row** Work 15 (17, 20) sts, with WS of pocket facing, work 32 sts from hold, work to end of row. Work in pattern for approximately 8", ending with row 8.

Place upper pocket

Work next 2 rows as for lower pocket. Work until Left Front matches Back length to underarm, ending with a WS row.

Shape armhole

Next row (RS) Bind off 10 sts at beginning of row (armhole edge), work to end of row. Work 1 row even. Decrease 1 st at armhole edge every RS row 10 times—43 (47, 53) sts. Work even until Left Front measures approximately 16 (18, 20)", ending with row 1 or 5.

Shape neck

Next row (WS) Bind off 10 sts (neck edge), work to end of row. Work 1 row even. **Next row** Bind off 3 sts at neck edge, work to end of row. Decrease 1 st at neck edge every RS row 7 (7, 10) times—23 (27, 30) sts. Work even until armhole measures approximately 8 (9, 9)", ending with row 1 or 5. Place all sts on hold.

RIGHT FRONT

Work as for Left Front to Shape armhole, **EXCEPT** end with a RS row.

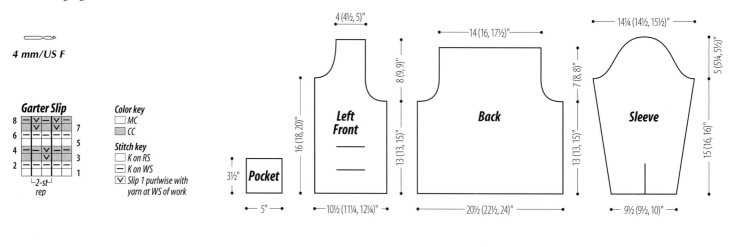

Garter Slip

8 | 7
6 | 5
4 | 3
2 | 1

2-st rep

Color key
☐ MC
▨ CC

Stitch key
☐ K on RS
— K on WS
☑ Slip 1 purlwise with yarn at WS of work

4 (4½, 5)"

Left Front

16 (18, 20)"

13 (13, 15)"

10½ (11¼, 12¼)"

3½"
Pocket
5"

14 (16, 17½)"

Back

8 (9, 9)"

13 (13, 15)"

20½ (22½, 24)"

14¼ (14½, 15½)"

7 (8, 8)"

Sleeve

5 (5¼, 5½)"

15 (16, 16)"

9½ (9½, 10)"

Shape armhole

Next row (WS) Bind off 10 sts at beginning of row (armhole edge), work to end of row. Decrease 1 st every RS row 10 times—43 (47, 53) sts. Work even until Front measures approximately 16 (18, 20)", ending with row 4 or 8.

Shape neck

Next row (RS) Bind off 10 sts (neck edge), work to end of row. Work 1 row even. *Next row* Bind off 3 sts at neck edge, work to end of row. Decrease 1 st at neck edge every RS row 7 (7, 10) times—23 (27, 30) sts. Work even until armhole measures approximately 8 (9, 9)", ending with row 4 or 8. Place all sts on hold.

SLEEVES
Cuffs

With MC, cast on 29 (29, 31) sts. P 1 row (WS). Work in Garter slip pattern for 4", ending with row 8, place sts on hold. Repeat from * to *, leaving sts on needle. *Next row* (RS) Work to 1 st remaining, k last st of piece together with first st of 2nd piece from hold, work all remaining sts from hold—57 (57, 61) sts. Increase 1 st at beginning and end of next RS row. Repeat increases every 8th row 13 (14, 15) more times—85 (87, 93) sts. Work even until Sleeve measures approximately 15 (16, 16)", ending with row 4 or 8.

Shape cap

Next row (RS) Bind off 10 sts at beginning of next 2 rows. Work 4 rows even. Decrease 1 st at beginning and end of next row. Repeat decreases every 4th row 4 more times, then every RS row until 13 (13, 15) sts remain. Bind off.

ASSEMBLY
Pocket trim

Row 1 With MC and RS facing, single crochet (sc) in each st—32 sc. Chain 1 (ch 1) and turn. *Row 2* 14 sc, ch 2 and skip 2 sc (buttonhole), 15 sc. Ch 1 and turn. *Row 3* 14 sc, work 2 sc in ch-2, 15 sc. Ch 1 and turn. *Row 4* *Sl st in 4 sts, ch 3; repeat from*, end sl st in 3 sts. Sew pocket linings in place.

Shoulders

With RS together and using MC, join Front and Back shoulder seams by binding off the 23 (27, 30) sts of one shoulder in 3-needle bind-off; bind off 37 (41, 45) back neck stitches; then bind off remaining 23 (27, 30) sts in 3-needle bind-off.

Seams

With MC and crochet slip st, set in sleeves, centering sleeve cap ½" forward from the shoulder seam, then join sleeve and side seams.

Sleeve cuff and placket trim

Right cuff Row 1 With MC and RS facing, starting at top of placket, sc down the front edge, across cuff, and up the back edge, working 3 sc in each corner, ch 1, turn. On front edge, mark for placement of 3 buttonholes, the first ½" above the lower edge of cuff, and the remaining two buttonholes spaced 1½" apart. *Row 2* Sc down back edge, across cuff, and up front edge, working 3 sc in each corner and working ch-3 buttonhole as for pockets where marked, ending with ch 1, turn. *Row 3* Sc in each sc and 3 sc in each buttonhole along front edge, 3 sc in corner, sc across cuff, ch 1, turn. *Row 4* *Sl st in 4 sts, ch 3, sl st in next st; repeat from* to end.

Left cuff Row 1 Work as right cuff **EXCEPT** begin sc along back edge. *Row 2* Sc down placket working buttonholes where marked, work 3 sc corner, sc across cuff to second corner, ch 1, turn. *Row 3* Sc across cuff, 3 sc in corner, sc in each sc and 3 sc in each buttonhole, ch 1, turn. *Row 4* Work as right cuff to second corner, slip st to top of placket.

Mark for buttons

Mark Left Front for 7 buttons, the top of one button about ½" down from the neck edge, the bottom of one button about 1" up from the bottom edge, the others equally spaced between. Mark Right Front for 7 matching buttonholes.

Neck, front, and bottom trim

Round 1 With MC, starting at right side seam, sc around, working 3 sc in corners. Join and ch 1. *Round 2* Sc around, working 3 sc in corners and placing buttonholes where indicated. Join and ch 1. *Round 3* Sc around, working 3 sc in corners and 2 sc in each buttonhole. Join and ch 1. *Round 4* *Sl st in 5 sts, ch 3; repeat from*. *Note* Adjust if necessary so ch-3 picots match along Fronts. Join. Block garment.

Make buttons

With MC, work sc over plastic ring until covered, join. Thread end of yarn in needle, sew into the sc opposite the join, then back into the last sc. Make a stitch perpendicular to this. Sew on buttons with CC.

Devonshire 10

Women's M: MC Brown, A Olive, B Gold

This tailored jacket, in a simple three-color stitch pattern, has the look of a textured tweed. For a more subtle fabric, try shades of gray, blue, or brown. The garment has a natural fit, neither too tight nor too loose, with slim, flattering sleeves. The four pockets and all edges are trimmed in a single color (the upper pockets can be eliminated if you wish). A neat collar finishes the neckline.

Devonshire

STANDARD FIT

FINISHED measurements

Women's S (M, L)
A 35½ (38½, 43)"
B 20½ (22½, 23½)"
C 26¾ (28¾, 31¼)"

10cm/4"

48 GET GAUGE!

24

over 3-color Tweed pattern

1 2 3 **4** 5 6

Medium weight
Main color (MC)
650 (750, 850) yds
Color A
500 (600, 700) yds
Color B
500 (600, 700) yds

Six ¾" buttons

4.5 mm/US 7
or size to obtain gauge

4 mm/US F

NOTES

1 See Techniques (page 96) for 3-needle bind-off, long-tail cast-on, loop cast-on (for buttonholes), buttonhole placement, and seam instructions. *2* Use long-tail cast-on except for buttonholes. *3* Work edge sts in Garter st (k every row). All increases and decreases are worked after the beginning edge st or before the ending edge st. *4* Carry contrasting colors not in use loosely up edge. *5* Slip all sts purlwise.

3-color Tweed pattern (multiple of 3 sts plus 1; includes edge sts)

Row 1 (RS) With A, k3, *slip 1 purlwise with yarn in back (sl 1 wyib), k2; repeat from*, end k1.
Row 2 With A, k3, *sl 1 purlwise with yarn in front (sl 1 wyif), k2; repeat from*, end k1.
Row 3 With B, *k2, sl 1 wyib; repeat from*, end k1.
Row 4 With B, k1, *sl 1 wyif, k2; repeat from*.
Row 5 With MC, k1, *sl 1 wyib, k2; repeat from*.
Row 6 With MC, k2, *sl 1 wyif, k2; repeat from*, end sl 1 wyif, k1.

BACK

With MC, cast on 109 (115, 130) sts. K1 row (WS). Work in 3-color Tweed pattern until Back measures 13 (14, 15)", ending with a WS row.

Shape armholes

Bind off 9 (9, 10) sts at beginning of next 2 rows. Decrease 1 st at beginning and end of every RS row 9 (9, 10) times—73 (79, 90) sts remain. Work even in pattern until armhole measures approximately 7 (8, 8)", ending with row 1. Place all sts on hold.

POCKET LININGS

Lower pocket (make 2)
With MC, cast on 28 sts. Work in St st (k on RS, p on WS) for 4". Place all sts on hold.

Upper pocket (make 2)
With MC, cast on 20 sts. Work in St st for 3". Place all sts on hold.

LEFT FRONT

With MC, cast on 58 (64, 70) sts. K1 row (WS). Work in 3-color Tweed pattern until Left Front measures approximately 5", ending with row 4.

Place lower pocket

Next row (RS) Continuing in pattern, work 16 (18, 22) sts, work next 28 sts and place on hold for pocket opening, work to end of row. *Next row* Work 14 (18, 20) sts, then with WS of lining facing, work in pattern across 28 sts of lower pocket lining, work to end of row. Work until Left Front matches Back length to armhole shaping, ending with a WS row.

Shape armhole

Next row (RS) Bind off 9 (9, 10) sts (armhole edge), work to end. Decrease 1 st at armhole edge every RS row 9 (9, 10) times—40 (46, 50) sts remain. Work even, ending with next row 4.

Place upper pocket

Next row (RS) Work 6 (8, 10) sts, work next 20 sts and place on hold for pocket opening, work to end of row. *Next row* Work 14 (18, 20) sts, then with WS of lining facing, work in pattern across 20 sts of upper pocket lining, work to end of row. Work until piece measures 17 (19, 21)" from beginning, ending with a RS row.

Shape neck

Next row (WS) Bind off 7 (10, 12) sts (neck edge), work to end of row. Work 1 row even. *Next row.* Bind off 3 sts, work to end of row. Work 1 row even. Decrease 1 st at neck edge every RS row 6 (7, 7) times—24 (26, 28) sts remain. Work even until armhole measures approximately 8 (9, 9)", ending with row 6. Place all sts on hold.

RIGHT FRONT

Work as for Left Front to Place lower pocket.

Place lower pocket

Work 14 (18, 20) sts, work next 28 sts and place on hold for pocket opening, work to end of row. *Next row* Work 16 (18, 22) sts, then with WS of lining facing, work in pattern across 28 sts of lower pocket lining, work to end of row. Work until Right Front matches Back length to armhole shaping, ending with a RS row.

Shape armhole

Next row (WS) Bind off 9 (9, 10) sts (armhole edge), work to end of row. Decrease 1 st at armhole edge every RS row 9 (9, 10) times—40 (46, 50) sts. Work even, ending with next row 4.

Place upper pocket

Next row (RS) Work 14 (18, 20) sts, work next 20 sts and place on hold for pocket opening, work to end of row. *Next row* Work 6 (8, 10) sts, then with WS of lining facing, work in pattern across 20 sts of upper pocket lining, work to end of row. Work until piece measures 17 (19, 21)" from beginning, ending with a WS row.

Shape neck

Next row (RS) Bind off 7 (10, 12) sts (neck edge), work to end of row. Work 1 row even. *Next row* (RS) Bind off 3 sts, work to end of row. Work 1 row even. Decrease 1 st at neck edge every RS row 6 (7, 7) times—24 (26, 28) sts remain. Work even until armhole measures approximately 8 (9, 9)", ending with row 6. Place all sts on hold.

SLEEVE

With MC, cast on 55 (58, 58) sts. K 1 row (WS). Work in 3-color Tweed pattern for 1". Increase 1 st at beginning and end of next RS row. Repeat increases every 1 (1, ¾)" on RS rows 14 (15, 21) times more—85 (90, 102) sts. Work even in pattern until sleeve measures 16 (17, 18)".

Shape cap

Bind off 9 (9, 10) sts at beginning of next 2 rows. Decrease 1 st at beginning and end of every RS row until 9 (10, 12) sts remain. Bind off.

COLLAR

With MC, cast on 85 (91, 97) sts. K 1 row (WS). Work in 3-color Tweed pattern for approximately 5", ending with row 6. With MC, k 1 row. Bind off.
Using MC, with RS facing, pick up and k 20 sts along each end of collar. K 1 row. Bind off.

ASSEMBLY

Pocket trim

With WS facing, k 1 row on sts from holder. Bind off. Sew pocket linings and ends of pocket trim in place.

Shoulders

With RS together and using MC, join Front and Back shoulder seams by binding off the 24 (26, 28) sts of one shoulder in 3-needle bind-off; bind off 25 (27, 34) Back neck stitches; then bind off remaining 24 (26, 28) sts in 3-needle bind-off.

Collar

Sew collar in place. Ends of collar should be placed approximately ½" in from center Front edges.

Left front edging

With MC and RS of Left Front facing, pick up and k 4 sts from collar to Front edge, and 84 (91, 98) sts along center Front edge. Knit 1 row. Bind off. Mark placement of 6 buttons: the top of one button ½" from top, the bottom of one button 3" from bottom, and the other 4 placed evenly between. Sew on buttons.

Right front edging

With MC and RS facing, pick up and k sts as worked on Left Front **EXCEPT** when you reach buttons, skip ¾" and cast on 3 sts using loop cast-on, ending with same number of sts as worked on Left Front. Pick up and knit 4 sts at neck edge, ending at collar. Knit 1 row. Bind off.

Seams

With crochet slip stitch and MC, set in sleeves, centering sleeve cap ½" forward from the shoulder seam, then join sleeve and side seams. Block garment.

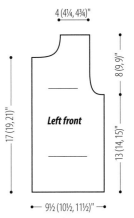

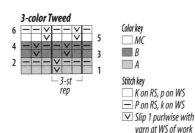

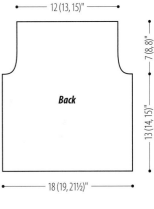

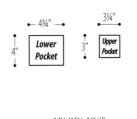

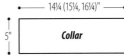

Atherton 11

So many knitters are afraid to combine yarns of different kinds or weights. Here, I combine two very different yarns, linen and mohair, in a slip-stitch pattern to create an interesting fabric. This combination has become one of my favorites. The style is Chanel with a stockinette border and pockets for interest.

Women's M: LOUET
Euroflax Sportweight - MC 3 skeins #16 Navy
Kid Mohair - CC Red

Atherton

Intermediate

STANDARD FIT

FINISHED measurements

Women's S (M, L)
A 40 (43½, 46½)"
B 20½ (21½, 23½)"
C 28¼ (30¼, 31¾)"

10cm/4"

48 **GET GAUGE!**
24

over Fabric stitch
using larger needles

1 2 **3** 4 5 6

Light weight
Main color (MC)
600 (700, 900) yds
Contrasting color (CC)
200 (300, 400) yds

Seven ¾" buttons
Two ½" buttons

2.75 mm/US 2
3.25 mm/US 3
or sizes to obtain gauges

4 mm/US F

NOTES

1 See Techniques (page 96) for 3-needle bind-off, one-row buttonholes, slip st, single crochet, and seam instructions. **2** Work edge sts in Garter st (k every row). All increases and decreases are worked after the beginning edge st or before the ending edge st. **3** Slip all sts purlwise.

Fabric stitch (multiple of 2 plus 1; includes edge sts)

Row 1 (RS) With MC, k.
Row 2 With MC, k.
Row 3 With CC, k2, *slip 1 purlwise with yarn in back (sl 1 wyib), k1; repeat from*, end k2.
Row 4 With CC, k2, *slip 1 purlwise with yarn in front (sl 1 wyif), k1; repeat from*, end k2.

BACK

With MC and smaller needles, cast on 109 (117, 129) sts. P 1 row (WS). Work 6 rows in St st (k on RS, p on WS). **Next row** (RS; fold line) *K2tog, yo; repeat from*, ending with yo, k1. Work 7 rows St st, increasing evenly across last row 14 (16, 16) sts—123 (133, 145) sts. **Next row** (RS) Change to larger needles and work even in Fabric st until Back measures approximately 13 (14, 15)" from fold line, ending with a WS row.

Shape armholes

Next row (RS) Bind off 10 sts at beginning of next 2 rows. Decrease 1 st at beginning and end of every RS row 6 (8, 8) times—91 (97, 109) sts. Work until armhole measures approximately 7 (7, 8)", ending with row 2. Place all sts on hold.

POCKET LININGS (make 2)

With CC and larger needles, cast on 27 sts and work in St st for 3". Place all sts on hold.

LEFT FRONT

With MC and smaller needles, cast on 57 (63, 67) sts. P 1 row (WS). Work same as Back, increasing 6 sts evenly on last row of St st—63 (69, 73) sts. **Next row** (RS) Change to larger needles and work even in Fabric st for 3½", ending with row 4.

Place pockets

Next row (RS) Work 18 (21, 23) sts, work next 27 sts and place on hold for pocket opening, work to end of row. **Next row** Work 18 (21, 23) sts, then with WS of lining facing, work in pattern across 27 sts of pocket lining, work to end of row. Work until Left Front matches Back length to underarm, ending with a WS row.

Shape armhole

Next row (RS) Bind off 10 sts (armhole edge), work to end of row. Work 1 row even. Decrease 1 st at armhole edge every RS row 6 (8, 8) times—47 (51, 55) sts. Work even until Left Front measures approximately 17 (18, 20)", ending with row 3.

Shape neck

Next row (WS) Bind off 10 (12, 12) sts (neck edge), work to end of row. Work 1 row even. **Next row** Bind off 3 sts, work to end of row. Decrease 1 st at neck edge every RS row 7 times—27 (29, 33) sts. Work even until armhole measures approximately 8 (8, 9)", ending with row 3. Place all sts on hold.

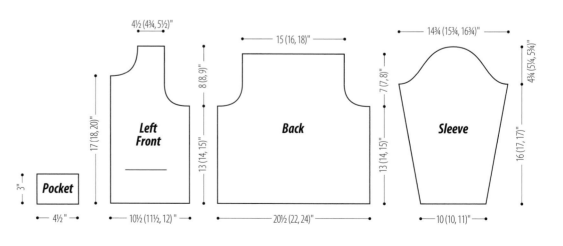

RIGHT FRONT

Work as for Left Front to underarm, ending with a RS row.

Shape armhole

Next row (WS) Bind off 10 sts (armhole edge), work to end of row. Decrease 1 st at armhole edge every RS row 6 (8, 8) times—47 (51, 55) sts. Work even until Right Front measures approximately 17 (18, 20)", ending with row 4.

Shape neck

Next row (RS) Bind off 10 (12, 12) sts (neck edge), work to end of row. Work 1 row even. **Next row** (RS) Bind off 3 sts, work to end of row. Decrease 1 st at neck edge every RS row 7 times—27 (29, 33) sts. Work even until armhole measures approximately 8 (8, 9)", ending with row 3. Place all sts on hold.

SLEEVES

With MC and smaller needles, cast on 55 (55, 57) sts. P1 row (WS). Work edging same as Back, increasing 6 (6, 8) sts evenly on last row of St st—61 (61, 65) sts. **Next row** (RS) Change to larger needles and Fabric st; work 8 rows. Increase 1 at beginning and end of next (RS) row. Repeat increases every 12 (8, 8)th row, 13 (16, 17) more times—89 (95, 101) sts. Work even until Sleeve measures 16 (17, 17)", from fold line, ending with row 4.

Shape cap

Next row (RS) Bind off 10 sts at beginning of next 2 rows. Decrease 1 st at beginning and end of every RS row until 11 (13, 13) sts remain. Bind off sts.

Fabric

Color key
☐ MC
▨ CC

Stitch key
☐ K on RS
⊟ K on WS
☑ Slip 1 purlwise with yarn at WS of work

ASSEMBLY

Pocket trim

With WS facing, using MC and smaller needles, k 1 row on sts from hold. **Next row** (RS) K1 row. **Next row** P12, k2tog, yo, p13. Work 2 more rows in St st. **Next row** (RS; fold line) *K2tog, yo; repeat from*, end k1. Work 2 rows St st. **Next row** P12, k2tog, yo, p13. K 1 row. Bind off. Sew pocket linings in place, fold trim to inside and sew in place, and overcast buttonholes. Sew on small buttons.

Shoulders

With RS together, join Front and Back shoulder seams by binding off the 27 (29, 33) sts of one shoulder in 3-needle bind-off; bind off 37 (39, 43) back neck sts; then bind off remaining 27 (29, 33) sts in 3-needle bind-off.

Neck edge

With RS facing and using MC and smaller needles, pick up and k approximately 80 (80, 90) sts on neck edge. K1 row. **Next row** (RS) Work 6 rows St st. **Next row** (RS; fold line) *K2tog, yo, repeat from*, ending yo, k1. Work 6 rows St st. Bind off.

Left Front edge

With MC and smaller needles, pick up and k approximately 108 (114, 120) sts on Left Front edge between upper and lower fold lines. Work as for Neck edge.

Button placement

Mark Left Front for large button placement with top of one button ½" below neck edge, bottom of one button 1" above bottom edge, and the remaining 5 buttons spaced equally between. Mark Right Front for matching buttonholes.

Right Front edge

With MC and smaller needles, repeat edge as for Left Front, **EXCEPT** where indicated on rows 4 and 12, work one-row buttonholes over 4 sts.
Fold all borders at fold line and sew in place.
Overcast buttonholes.

Seams

With crochet slip st, set in sleeves, centering sleeve cap ½" forward from the shoulder seam, then join sleeve and side seams. Sew on buttons.
Block garment.

Winchester 12

Linen stitch makes a most interesting fabric with a woven look. In this jacket I used three soft colors of a lightweight yarn. Linen stitch makes a dense fabric, so the yarn should be lightweight. With the focus on the fabric, the detailing can be kept to a minimum. A simple collar frames the V-neck; there are no pockets and no buttons. If you wish to keep the jacket closed, a hidden button with a chain loop could be placed on the inside. This jacket is short, but that is a personal choice; make it longer if you wish.

Women's M: LION BRAND
Wool-Ease Sportweight - 2 balls each:

MC #152 Oxford Grey
A #139 Dark Rose Heather
B #098 Natural Heather

Winchester

Intermediate

STANDARD FIT

FINISHED measurements

Women's S (M, L)
A 39½ (42½, 46)"
B 19½ (20½, 22½)"
C 28 (29¾, 31¼)"

10cm/4"

48 | GET GAUGE!
28

over Linen pattern

1 **2** 3 4 5 6

Fine weight
Main color (MC)
Color A
Color B
550 (600, 650) yds each color

One ¾" clear button

4.5 mm/US 7
or size to obtain gauge

4 mm/US F

NOTES

1 See Techniques (page 96) for long-tail cast-on, 3-needle bind-off, ssk, single crochet, and seam instructions. *2* Work edge sts in Garter st (k every row). All increases and decreases are done after the beginning edge st or before the ending edge st. *3* Yarn color changes after every row. *4* Carry contrasting colors not in use loosely up edge. *5* Slip all sts purlwise.

Linen pattern (Multiple of 2; includes edge sts)
Row 1 (RS) With B, k1, *k1, slip 1 st purlwise with yarn in front (sl 1 wyif); repeat from*, k1.
Row 2 With A, k1, *p1, sl 1 purlwise with yarn in back (sl 1 wyib); repeat from*, k1.
Row 3 With MC, repeat row 1.
Row 4 With B, repeat row 2.
Row 5 With A, repeat row 1.
Row 6 With MC, repeat row 2.

BACK

With MC, cast on 140 (150, 160) sts. P 1 row (WS). Work in Linen pattern until Back measures approximately 12 (13, 14)", ending with a WS row.

Shape armholes

Bind off 10 sts at beginning of next 2 rows. Decrease 1 st at beginning and end of every RS row 11 (13, 13) times—98 (104, 114) sts remain. Work even until the armhole measures 7 (7, 8)", ending with a WS row. Place all sts on hold.

LEFT FRONT

With MC, cast on 70 (76, 82) sts. P 1 row (WS). Work in Linen pattern until Left Front matches Back length to underarm, ending with WS row.

Shape armhole and neck

Next row (RS) Bind off 10 sts (armhole edge), work to end of row. Work 1 row even. *Next row* (RS) Decrease 1 st at beginning of row, work to 3 sts remaining and k2tog, k1 (neck edge). Decrease 1 st at armhole every RS row 10 (12, 12) more times, **AT SAME TIME,** decrease 1 st at neck edge every 4th row 16 (17, 20) more times—32 (35, 38) sts. Work even until armhole measures 8 (8, 9)", ending with a WS row. Place all sts on hold.

RIGHT FRONT

Work same as Left Front to underarm, ending with a RS row.

Shape armhole and neck

Next row (WS) Bind off 10 sts (armhole edge), work to end of row. *Next row* (RS) K1, ssk, (neck edge) work to 2 sts remaining and decrease 1 st at armhole edge. Work 1 row even. Decrease 1 st at armhole edge every RS row 10 (12, 12) more times, **AT SAME TIME,** decrease 1 st at neck edge every 4th row 16 (17, 20) more times—32 (35, 38) sts. Work even until armhole measures 8 (8, 9)", ending with a WS row. Place all sts on hold.

SLEEVES

With MC, cast on 68 (68, 72) sts. P 1 row (WS). Work in Linen pattern for 1", ending with a WS row.

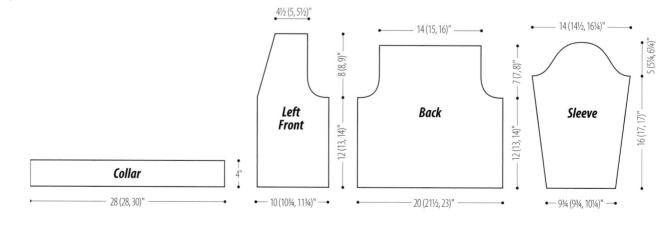

Increase 1 st at beginning and end of next RS row. Repeat increases every 12(8, 8)th row, 14 (16, 20) more times—98 (102, 114) sts. Work even until Sleeve measures 16 (17, 17)", ending with a WS row.

Shape cap
Bind off 10 sts at beginning of next 2 rows. Decrease 1 st at beginning and end of every RS row until 18 (18, 20) sts remain. Bind off sts.

COLLAR
With MC, cast on 196 (196, 210) sts. P 1 row (WS). Work in Linen pattern for 4". Bind off. With MC, work 1 row of single crochet on side edges of collar.

ASSEMBLY
Shoulders
With RS together and using MC, join Front and Back shoulder seams by binding off the 32 (35, 38) sts of one shoulder in 3-needle bind-off; bind off 34 (34, 38) back neck stitches; then bind off remaining 32 (35, 38) sts in 3-needle bind-off.

Collar
Sew collar to jacket, with ends at starting points of V-neck shaping, and middle centered at back neck. With MC, work 1 row of single crochet on front edges of jacket.

Seams
With crochet slip stitch and MC, set in sleeves, centering sleeve cap ½" forward from the shoulder seam; then join sleeve and side seams. Block garment.

Closure(optional)
On WS of Right Front edge, work chain-3 loop at waist. Sew a small flat button on WS of Left Front edge.

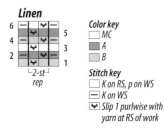

Linen

Color key
☐ MC
▨ A
▨ B

Stitch key
☐ K on RS, p on WS
— K on WS
☒ Slip 1 purlwise with yarn at RS of work

Boylston 13

Some yarns have it all: great texture, gorgeous color, even a touch of glitz. They need to be treated like a lovely picture— framed to show off their beauty. The stitch pattern used here nicely achieves that goal. The jacket's silhouette is straight, with a fullness that provides ease without bulk. The square neckline echoes the grid lines of the color pattern. Slit pockets are placed above the hip. For those who wish to make a suit, I also designed an easy skirt pattern.

Jacket, Women's L: TRENDSETTER
Dune - MC 10 balls #68
Lane Borgosesia Merino Otto - CC 4 balls #25278 Olive

Skirt, Women's M: TRENDSETTER
Lane Borgosesia Merino Otto - 7 balls #25278 Olive

Boylston

JACKET
NOTES

1 See Techniques (page 96) for 3-needle bind-off, long-tail cast-on, one-row buttonhole, buttonhole placement, and seam instructions. *2* Use long-tail cast-on except for buttonholes. *3* Work edge sts in Garter st (k every row). All increases and decreases are worked after the beginning edge st or before the ending edge st. *4* Carry contrasting colors not in use loosely up edge. *5* Slip all sts purlwise.

Body pattern (multiple of 6 plus 3; includes edge sts)
Row 1 (WS) With CC, k1, p across row, end k1.
Row 2 With MC, k.
Row 3 With MC, k1, p across row, end k1.
Row 4 Repeat Row 2.
Row 5 Repeat Row 3.
Row 6 With CC, k4, *k into CC st 5 rows down and drop sts above, k5; repeat from*, end last repeat k4.

BACK

With CC, cast on 81 (93, 99, 105) sts. K 4 rows, ending with a RS row. Work in Body pattern until Back measures 12 (13, 14, 15)", ending with a WS row.

Shape armholes

Bind off 6 (8, 8, 10) sts at beginning of next 2 rows. Decrease 1 st at beginning and end of every RS row 5 (7, 7, 6) times—59 (63, 69, 73) sts. Work even until armhole measures approximately 7 (7, 8, 8)", ending with row 6. Place all sts on hold.

POCKET LININGS (make 2)

With CC, cast on 25 sts. Work in St st (k on RS, p on WS) for 3¾", ending with a WS row. Place all sts on hold.

LEFT FRONT

With CC, cast on 45 (51, 57, 63) sts. K 4 rows, ending with a RS row. Work in Body pattern for approximately 4½", ending with row 6.

Place pocket

Next row (RS) Work 10 (13, 16, 19) sts, then work 25 sts and place on hold, work 10 (13, 16, 19) sts. *Next row* Work 10 (13, 16, 19) sts, then with WS of lining facing, work in pattern across 25 sts of pocket lining, work to end of row. Work even until Left Front matches Back length to underarm, ending with a WS row.

Shape armhole

Bind off 7 (7, 9, 10) sts at beginning of next row (armhole edge). Work 1 row even. Decrease 1 st at armhole edge every RS row 7 (6, 8, 8) times—31 (38, 40, 45) sts. Work even until Front measures approximately 17 (18, 20, 21)", ending with row 6.

Shape neck

Bind off 12 (18, 18, 23) sts at beginning of row (neck edge). Continue in pattern on 19 (20, 22, 22) sts until armhole measures approximately 8 (8, 9, 9)", ending with row 6. Place all sts on hold.

RIGHT FRONT

Work as for Left Front to underarm **EXCEPT** end with a RS row.

Shape armhole

Bind off 7 (7, 9, 10) sts at beginning of next row (armhole edge). Decrease 1 st at armhole edge every RS row 7 (6, 8, 8) times—31 (38, 40, 45) sts. Work even until Right Front measures 17 (18, 20, 21)", ending with row 6.

Shape neck

Bind off 12 (18, 18, 23) sts at beginning of row (neck edge). Continue in pattern on 19 (20, 22, 22) sts until

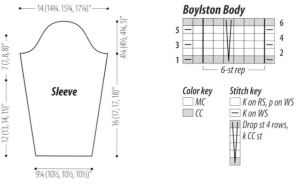

Left Front

Pocket

Back

Sleeve

Boylston Body

6-st rep

Color key
☐ MC
▨ CC

Stitch key
☐ K on RS, p on WS
⊟ K on WS
▨ Drop st 4 rows, k CC st

armhole measures approximately 8 (8, 9, 9)", ending with row 6. Place all sts on hold.

SLEEVES

With CC, cast on 39 (45, 45, 45) sts. K 4 rows, ending with a RS row. Work in Body pattern for 6 rows. Increase 1 st at beginning and end of next (RS) row and every 8th row 9 (8, 10, 13) more times—59 (63, 67, 73) sts. Work even until Sleeve measures 16 (17, 17, 18)", ending with a WS row.

Shape cap

Bind off 6 (7, 8,10) sts at beginning of next 2 rows. Decrease 1 st at beginning and end of every RS row until 13 sts remain. Bind off all sts.

ASSEMBLY

Pocket trim

With RS of Left Front facing, place sts from hold on needle. With CC, k 4 rows. Bind off. Sew pocket linings and ends of trim in place. Repeat for Right Front.

Shoulders

With RS together and using CC, join Front and Back shoulder seams by binding off the 19 (20, 22, 22) sts of one shoulder in 3-needle bind-off; bind off 21 (23, 25, 29) back neck stitches; then bind off remaining 19 (20, 22, 22) sts in 3-needle bind-off.

Neck edge

With CC and RS facing, pick up and k12 (18, 18, 23) sts on right front neck, place marker (pm), k15 sts along side of neck, 21 (23, 25, 29) sts across back of neck, pm, 15 sts along side of neck and 12 (18, 18, 23) for left front neck—75 (89, 91, 105) sts. K 1 row. **Next row** (RS) *K to 1 st before marker, k2tog; repeat from*, k to end. Work 1 row even. Repeat last 2 rows. Bind off.

Button placement

Mark placement of buttons on Left Front: the top of one button ½" from top edge, and the bottom of one

Waistband casing

button 3" from bottom, with remaining 3 buttons placed evenly between. Sew on buttons. Mark Right Front for matching buttonholes.

Front bands

Left front band With CC and RS facing, pick up and k approximately 100 (106, 112, 118) sts along center Front edge. K 4 rows. Bind off.
Right front band With CC and RS facing, pick up and k same number of sts as on Left Front. K 1 row. **Next row** (RS) K, working one-row buttonholes over 4 sts where indicated. K 2 rows. Bind off.

Seams

With crochet slip stitch and MC, set in sleeves, centering sleeve cap ½" forward from shoulder seam, then join sleeve and side seams. Block garment.

SKIRT
NOTES

1 See Techniques (page 96) for lifted increases and single crochet. *2* Work lifted increase for all increases.

Cast on 168 (180, 192, 204, 216) sts, place marker (pm), join, taking care that cast-on sts are not twisted. Work in the round in k1, p1 ribbing for 84 (90, 96, 102, 108) sts, pm for side seam, and work rib to end of round. Continue in k1, p1 ribbing for 1". Change to St st (k all sts, all rounds) and work 1". **Next round** *K23 (25, 26, 27, 28), pm, k38 (40, 44, 48, 52), pm, k23 (25, 26, 27, 28); repeat from*.

Increase rounds

K1, increase 1, *k to marker, increase 1, k1, increase 1; repeat from*, ending last repeat k to marker, increase 1—180 (192, 204, 216, 228) sts. Repeat increases every 1" 6 times more—252 (264, 276, 288, 300) sts. Work even until Skirt measures 21 (22, 23, 24, 25)", or desired length. Bind off loosely.

Bottom edging

Work 3 rounds of single crochet around bind-off edge. At end of each round, join with a slip st then chain 1.

Waistband

Make casing for elastic waistband (see illustration), place elastic in casing and sew ends together to fit waist. Block garment.

Easy

B | A
STANDARD FIT

FINISHED measurements

Women's S (M, L, XL, XXL)
A 42 (44, 46, 48, 50)"
B 21½ (22½, 23½, 24½, 25½)"
C 28 (30, 32, 34, 36)"

10cm/4"

28 | GET GAUGE!
24

over Stockinette stitch

1 2 **3** 4 5 6

Light weight
900 (950, 1050, 1150, 1250) yds

3.75 mm/US 5 - 24" circular
or size to obtain gauge

3.75 mm/US E

&

One yard 1" elastic
for waistband

28 (30, 32, 34, 36)"

21 (22, 23, 24, 25)"

Skirt

42 (44, 46, 48, 50)"

Sanquar 14

The beauty of handpainted
yarns inspired this jacket.
I used a slip-stich block
pattern to display the
changing colors against
a solid background. The
blocks richest in color and
texture are arranged to
border the edges of this
jacket. The colors truly
shine! Now to try this idea
with a dark background.

Women's M: SCHAEFER YARNS
Helene - MC 14 ounces Natural, CC 1 skein multicolor colorway

Sanquar

Advanced

STANDARD FIT

FINISHED measurements
Women's S (M, L)
A 37 (41, 44)"
B 17¾ (19¼, 20½)"
C 27 (28½, 30)"

10cm/4"

48 **GET GAUGE!**
24

over Cross Block pattern

1 2 3 **4** 5 6

Medium weight
Main color (MC)
900 (1000, 1200) yds
Contrasting color (CC)
500 (600, 700) yds

Twelve (twelve, thirteen)
¾" buttons

4.5 mm/US 7 - 24" circular
or size to obtain gauge

4 mm/US F

NOTES

1 See Techniques (page 96) for 3-needle bind-off, crab st, and seam instructions. *2* Work 1 edge st in Garter st each side (k every row). All increases and decreases are worked after the beginning edge st or before the ending edge st. *3* Sl all sts purlwise. *4* Each block pattern is a multiple of 4 plus 1. Because the two block patterns are combined throughout the jacket, you will only place one "plus 1" stitch at the end of RS rows and beginning of WS rows. (M will not use the "plus 1" after armhole shaping because of the half blocks.)

Cross Block pattern (Multiple of 4 plus 1) - (Block A)
Row 1 (RS) With MC, *(sl1 with yarn in back (wyib), k1) 2 times, repeat from*, end sl1.
Row 2 With MC, *(sl1 with yarn in front (wyif), p1) 2 times, repeat from* end sl1.
Row 3 With CC, k.
Row 4 With CC, k.
Row 5 With MC, repeat row 1.
Row 6 With MC, repeat row 2.
Row 7 With CC, k.
Row 8 With CC, k.

Blank Block pattern (Multiple of 4 plus 1) - (Block B)
Row 1 (RS) With MC, *(sl1 wyib, k3), repeat from* end sl1.
Row 2 With MC, *(sl1 wyif, p3), repeat from* end sl1.
Row 3 With CC, *(k1, sl3 wyib), repeat from* k1.

Row 4 With CC, *(k1, sl3 wyif), repeat from*, end k1.
Row 5 With MC, repeat row 1.
Row 6 With MC, repeat row 2.
Row 7 With CC, k.
Row 8 With CC, k.

POCKET LININGS (Make 2)
With CC, cast on 24 sts. Work in St st (k on RS, p on WS) for 3½". Place all sts on hold.

BODY
Border
With CC, cast on 223 (247, 263). K 1 row. *Next 8 rows* Starting on (RS) K1 (edge st), *work 1 block (A), work 1 block (B), repeat from* to end with (A), k1. *Next 8 rows* K1, **work 1 (B), 1 (A), repeat from ** end with k1. Repeat these 16 rows 2 more times, ending with row 6.

Pocket placement
Continuing in pattern, work 25 (25, 33) sts, work next 24 sts and place on hold for pocket opening, work 125 (149, 149) sts, work 24 sts and place on hold, work 25 (25, 33) sts to end of row. *Next row* Work 25 (25, 33) sts, then, with WS of lining facing, work in pattern across 24 sts of pocket lining, work to second hold and work second pocket lining, work to end of row.

Front border and body
Next 8 rows (RS) K1, work 1 (A), 1 (B), 1 (A), then work 49 (55, 59) (B), 1 (A), 1 (B), 1 (A), k1. *Next 8 rows* K1, *1 (B), 1 (A) 2 times, then work 47(53, 57) (B), *1 (A), 1 (B), repeat from* 2 times, k1. Repeat these 16 rows 4 more times to underarm, ending with row 8.

Block A
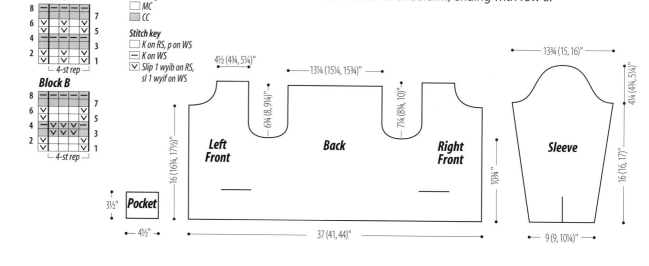

Color key
☐ MC
▨ CC

Stitch key
☐ K on RS, p on WS
☐ K on WS
☑ Slip 1 wyib on RS, sl 1 wyif on WS

Divide for underarms

Continuing in Front border and body pattern as established, work 50 (55, 58) sts in pattern as established and place on hold, bind off 15 (17, 19) sts, work 93 (103, 109) sts and place on hold, bind off 15 (17, 19) sts, work 50 (55, 58) sts to end of row.

LEFT FRONT

Continuing in pattern, work 1 row even. At armhole edge, decrease 1 st on every RS row 7 (6, 7) times—43 (49, 51) sts. *MEDIUM has two extra sts at armhole edge; treat them as a half block.* Continue until 4 (6, 6) blocks completed above armhole bind off.

Next 8 rows (RS) K1, work 5 (6½, 7) (B), *1 (A), 1 (B), repeat from* 1 more time, end with (A), k1.

Next 8 rows K1, work 4 (5½, 6) (B), *1 (A), 1 (B), repeat from* 2 more times, k1.

Next 8 rows K1, work 3 (4½, 5) (B), *1 (A), 1 (B), repeat from* 2 more times, 1 (A), k1, ending with row 7 for Medium.

S and L ONLY: Next 8 rows K1, work 2 (0, 4) (B), *1(A), 1 (B), repeat from* 3 more times, k1, ending with row 7 for Small.

L ONLY: Next 8 rows (RS) K1, work 0 (0, 3) (B), *1 (A), 1 (B), repeat from* 3 more times, end with 1 (A), k1, ending with Row 7 for Large.

Shape Neck

Note: Work extra stitches into block pattern.

Next row Bind off 11 (13, 13) sts at neck edge, work to end of row.

Next 8 rows K1, 1 (3½, 2) (B), *1 (A), 1 (B) repeat from* to end of row, **AT SAME TIME**, decrease 1 st at neck edge every RS row 5 (7, 7) times—27 (29, 31) sts.

Next 8 rows K1, 0 (2½, 1) (B),*1 (A), 1 B), repeat from* to end of row, k1.

Next 8 rows K1, work 1 (1½, 0) (B), *1 (A), 1 (B) repeat from* to end of row, k1. Place all sts on hold for Small.

For Medium and Large ONLY:

Next 8 rows K1, work 0 (½, 1) (B), *1 (A), 1 (B), repeat from* to end of row, k1. Work to row 7. Place all sts on hold.

BACK

Join yarn at left side underarm and work 1 row in pattern. Continue in (B), decrease 1 st at beginning and end of every RS row 7 (6, 7) times—79 (91, 95) sts.

MEDIUM has half blocks on each side.

Work even until 7 (9, 11) blocks (B) completed above armhole.

Back Yoke pattern

Next 8 rows K1, work 2(3½, 2) (B), then *work 1 (A), 1 (B), repeat from* 7 (7, 9) more times, ending with 1(2½, 1) (B), k1.

Next 8 rows K1, work 1 (2½, 1) (B), then *work 1 (A), 1 (B), repeat from* 8 (8, 10) more times, ending with 0 (1½, 0) (B), k1.

Next 8 rows K1, Work 0 (1½, 0) (B), then *work 1 (A), 1 (B), repeat from* 8 (9, 10) more times, ending with 1 (0, 1) (A), 0 (½, 0) (B) k1. End with row 7. Place all sts on hold.

⊞ *Block A*
☐ *Block B*

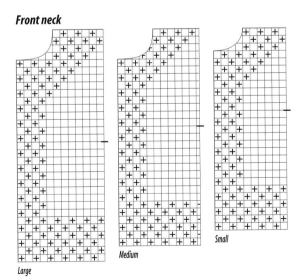

Front neck

Small

Medium

Large

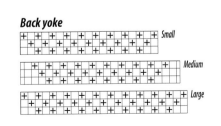

Back yoke

Small

Medium

Large

Sanquar

RIGHT FRONT

Join yarn at underarm and work 1 row in pattern. At armhole edge, decrease 1 sts on every RS row, 7 (6, 7) times—43 (49, 51) sts. **Medium has extra stitches on edge; treat them as a half block.** Continue until 4 (6, 6) blocks completed above armhole bind-off.

Next 8 rows (RS) K1, *1 (A), 1 (B), repeat from* 1 more time, 1 (A), end with 5 (6½, 7) (B), k1.

Next 8 rows K1, *1 (B), 1 (A), repeat from* 2 more times, work 4 (5½, 6) (B), k1.

Next 8 rows K1, *1 (A), 1 (B), repeat from* 2 more times, 1 (A), 3 (4½, 5) (B), k1, ending row 8 for Medium.

S and L ONLY: Next 8 rows K1, *1 (B), 1 (A), repeat from* 3 more times, work 2 (0, 4) (B), k1, ending with row 8 for Small.

L ONLY: Next 8 rows (RS) K1, *1 (A), 1 (B), repeat from* 1 more time, end with 1 (A), 0 (0, 3) (B), k1, ending with row 8 for Large.

Shape Neck
NOTE

Work partial blocks at neck to correspond to fabric pattern.

Next 8 rows Bind off 11 (13,13) sts at neck edge, K1, work 1 (0, 2) (B), *1 (A), 1 (B), repeat from* 1 more time, 1 (A), 1 (3½, 2) (B), k1.

AT SAME TIME, decrease 1 st at neck edge every RS row 5 (7, 7) times—27 (29, 31) sts.

Next 8 rows K1, 1 (0, 1) (B),*1 (A), 1 (B), repeat from* 1 more time, 1 (A), 0 (2½, 1) (B), k1.

Next 8 rows K1, 0 (1, 0) (B),*1 (A), 1 (B) repeat from* 2 more times, 1 (A), 1 (1½, 0) (B), k1. Work to row 7, place all sts on hold for Small.

For Medium and Large ONLY:
Next 8 rows K1, 0 (1, 0) (A), *1 (B), 1 (A), repeat from* 3 more times, 0 (½, 1) (B), k1. Work to row 7 and place all sts on hold.

SLEEVES

Increases are placed at sleeve edges. Work them into block B pattern repeats as the fabric is knit.

Right half of cuff

With CC, cast on 27 (27, 31) sts. K 1 row.

Next 8 rows (RS) K1, 0 (0, 1) (B) *1 (B), 1 (A), repeat from* 2 more times, k1.

Next 8 rows K1, 0 (0, 1) (B)*1 (A), 1 (B), repeat from*, 2 more times, k1.

Next 8 rows K1, 5 (5, 6) (B), 1 (A), k1. Increase 1 st at beginning of row 8, working extra stitches as necessary to maintain pattern.

Next 8 rows K1, 4 (4, 5) (B), 1 (A), 1 (B), k1.

Next 8 rows K1, 5 (5, 6) (B), 1 (A), k1 end with row 7. Place all sts on hold.

Left half of cuff

With CC, cast on 27 (27, 31) sts. K 1 row.

Next 8 rows (RS) K1, *1 (A), 1 (B), repeat from* 2 more times, 0(0, 1)(A), k1.

Next 8 rows K1, *1 (B), 1 (A), repeat from* 2 more times, 0(0, 1)(B) k1.

Next 8 rows K1, 1 (A), 5 (5, 6) (B), k1. Increase 1 st at end row 8, working extra stitches as necessary to maintain pattern.

Next 8 rows K1, 1 (B), 1 (A), 4 (4, 5) (B), k1.

Next 8 rows K1, 1 (A), 5 (5, 6) (B), k1 end with row 7. Work row 8, increase 1 at beginning, work across, cast on 1 st and work stitches of right half cuff, increase 1—59(59, 67) sts.

Next 8 rows K1, 6 (6, 7) (B), 1 (A), 6 (6, 7) (B), k1. Continue working in (B), increasing 1 st at beginning and end of every 8 (10, 10)th row 10 (15, 15) times more—79 (89, 97) sts. Work even until Sleeve measures 16 (17, 17)", ending with a WS row.

Shape cap

Bind off 8 (9, 10) sts at beginning of next 2 rows. Decrease 1 st at beginning and end of every RS row 26 (29, 32) times. Bind off 10 (11, 14) sts.

Cuff

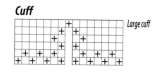

Large cuff

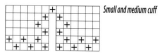

Small and medium cuff

ASSEMBLY

Shoulders

With RS together, using MC, join Front and Back shoulder seams by binding off 27 (29, 31) sts of one shoulder in 3-needle bind-off; bind off 25 (33, 33) back neck sts; then bind off remaining 27 (29, 31) sts in 3-needle bind-off.

Left front edging

With RS of Left front facing, using CC, pick up 92 (108, 120) sts, k2 rows. Bind off.

Mark buttonholes

Mark placement for 6 (6, 7) Buttons on Left front, the first, ½" from top, the last 2" from bottom, the remaining buttons spaced evenly between. Mark buttonhole spacing on Right front to correspond to Left front buttons.

Right front edging

With RS of Right front facing, using CC, pick up 92 (108, 120) sts. K to buttonhole marker, work 1 row buttonhole over 3 sts, repeat for remaining buttonholes, taking care to keep same number of sts between each buttonhole. K 1 row. Bind off.

Collar

With CC, and RS facing, starting at top of right side neck, pick up 87 (95, 95) sts around neck. K 3 rows. *Next 8 rows* (RS) K1, *1 (B), 1 (A), repeat from*, ending with 1 (B), k1. Break yarn. *Next row* With CC, pick up and K6 sts along front edge of collar, k collar sts, pick up and k6 sts on edge. K 1 row and bind off.

Seams

With crochet slip st set in sleeves, centering sleeve cap ½" forward from the shoulder seam, then crochet slip st sleeve and side seams.

Cuffs

With CC, pick up 25 sts along back edge of cuff and k 2 rows. Bind off. Mark for placement of 3 buttons. On Front edge of cuff, pick up 25 sts. Make 1 row buttonholes over 3 sts as for Front edge. K 1 row. Bind off. Block garment. Sew on buttons.

Stuart 15

I designed this jacket a few years ago using the stitch pattern featured on the cover of Mary Walker Phillips' book of knitted counterpanes. When I saw this stitch, I knew I had to use it in a jacket. I have worn my jacket shopping, to luncheons, and in the evenings to dinner and the theater. I love its versatility.

Women's M/L: BROWN SHEEP
Naturespun Sportweight - 9 balls #48 Scarlet

Stuart

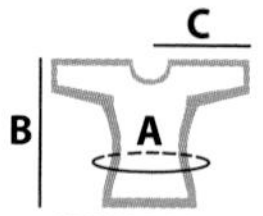

STANDARD FIT

FINISHED measurements

Women's XS/S (M/L)
A 36¾ (45¾)"
B 17¾ (19¼)"
C 27 (28½)"

10cm/4"

36 | **GET GAUGE!**
28

over Scalloped pattern

1 2 **3** 4 5 6

Light weight
1800 (2200) yds

Ten (eleven) ¾" buttons

3.5 mm/US 4
or size to obtain gauge

4 mm/US F

&

1 double-pointed needle

NOTES

1 See Techniques (page 96) for 3-needle bind-off, ssk, long-tail cast-on, loop cast-on (for buttonholes), buttonhole placement, and seam instructions. *2* Use long-tail cast-on except for buttonholes. *3* Work edge sts in Garter st (k every row). All increases and decreases are worked after the beginning edge st or before the ending edge st. *4* Slip all sts purlwise.

P4-wrap P4 sts, place on a double-pointed or cable needle and wrap yarn counterclockwise around the four sts. Wrap 3 times; return the four sts to the right-hand needle and continue.

Scalloped pattern (Begins with multiple of 21 plus 5 sts; includes edge sts)
Row 1, 3 (WS) K.
Row 2 K1, p across, end k1.
Row 4 K2, *yo, k21; repeat from*, end k3.
Row 5 K1, p3, *(k3, p1) 5 times, p2; repeat from*, end k1.
Row 6 K3, *yo, k1, (p3, k1) 5 times, yo, k1; repeat from*, end k2.
Row 7 K1, *p4, (k3, p1) 5 times; repeat from*, end p3, k1.
Row 8 K3, *yo, k1, yo, (ssk, p2) 5 times, (k1, yo) 2 times, k1; repeat from*, end k2.
Row 9 K1, *p6, (k2, p1) 5 times, p2; repeat from*, end p3, k1.
Row 10 K3, *(yo, k1) 3 times, yo, (ssk, p1) 5 times, (k1, yo) 4 times, k1; repeat from*, end k2.
Row 11 K1, *p10, (k1, p1) 5 times, p6; repeat from*, end p3, k1.
Row 12 K2, *k8, (ssk) 5 times, k8; repeat from*, end k3.
Row 13 K1, *p10, p4-wrap, p7; repeat from*, end p3, k1.
Row 14 K all sts.

BACK

Cast on 131 (152) sts. Work in Scalloped pattern until Back measures approximately 9¼ (10¾)", ending with row 13.
Shape armholes
Bind off 21 sts at beginning of next 2 rows—89 (110) sts. Work even until armhole measures

approximately 8", ending with Row 3. Place all sts on hold.

LEFT FRONT

Cast on 68 (89) sts. Work in Scalloped pattern until Left Front matches Back length to underarm, ending with row 13.
Shape armhole
Bind off 21 sts at beginning of next row (armhole edge)—47 (68) sts. Work even until Left Front measures approximately 15½ (17)", ending with Row 14.
Shape neck
Next row (WS) Bind off 11 (22) sts at beginning of row (neck edge), work to end of row. Work 1 row even. *Next row* Bind off 3 sts, work to end of row. Work 1 row even. Work ssk at neck edge every RS row 7 times—26 (36) sts. Work even until armhole measures approximately 9¼", ending with row 14. Place all sts on hold.

RIGHT FRONT

Work as for Left Front to underarm, EXCEPT ending with row 14.
Shape armhole
Bind off 21 sts at beginning of next row (armhole edge)—47 (68) sts. Work even until Left Front measures approximately 15½ (17)", ending with Row 13.
Shape neck
Next row (RS) Bind off 11 (22) sts at beginning of row (neck edge), work to end of row. Work 1 row even. *Next row* Bind off 3 sts, work to end of row. Work 1 row even. K2tog at neck edge every RS row 7 times—26 (36) sts.

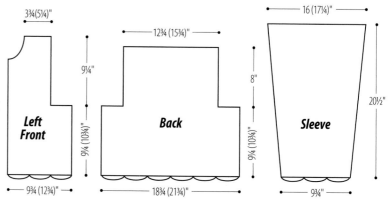

3¾(5¼)"

12¾ (15¾)"

16 (17¼)"

9¼"

8"

15½ (17)"

Left Front

9¼ (10¾)"

Back

9¼ (10¾)"

Sleeve

20½"

9¾ (12¾)"

18¾ (21¾)"

9¾"

Work even until armhole measures approximately 9¼" ending with row 14. Place all sts on hold.

SLEEVES

Cast on 68 (68) sts. Work in Scalloped pattern for 3 rows. ***Next row*** (RS)Increase 1 st at beginning and end of next row. Keeping all increased sts in reverse St st (p on RS, k on WS), repeat increases every 6th row 21 (25) more times—112 (120) sts. Work even until Sleeve measures approximately 20½", or length desired, ending with row 3. Place sts on hold.

ASSEMBLY

Shoulders

With RS together, join Front and Back shoulder seams by binding off the 26 (36) sts of one shoulder in 3-needle bind-off; bind off 37 (38) Back neck stitches; then bind off remaining 26 (36) sts in 3-needle bind-off.

Left Front edging

With RS facing, starting at top of Left Front edge, pick up and k 120 (130) sts. Work 3 rows reverse St st. Bind off.

Buttonhole placement

On Left Front, mark for placement of 10 (11) buttons, the first just below neck edge, and one button at each reverse St st ridge. Mark Right Front for buttonholes to correspond to buttons.

Right Front Edging and Buttonholes

With RS facing, starting at bottom of Right Front edge, pick up and k 120 (130) sts **EXCEPT** when you reach buttonhole location, *cast on 3 sts using loop cast-on, skip 3 sts; repeat from* at each buttonhole. Work 3 rows reverse St st. Bind off. Sew on buttons.

Neck edge

With RS facing, pick up and k 100 (112) sts around neck edge. Work as for Front edges and bind off.

Join Sleeves

With RS facing, pick up and k 112 (120) sts along armhole edge. With RS together, join Sleeve to Body by binding off in 3-needle bind-off.

Seams

With crochet slip st, join sleeve and side seams. Block garment.

Stitch key
☐ K on RS, p on WS
▨ P on RS, k on WS
◦ Yo
◥ Ssk
▬ Purl 4 wrap
■ Skip to next square

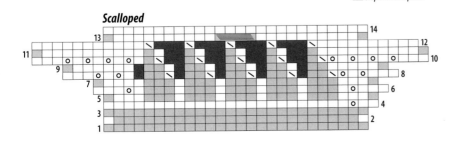

Scalloped

Clarendon 16

I wanted to explore the possibility of knitting a double-breasted jacket—a strong jacket, without frills and yet with a unique look. This twill is a good choice: it yields a strong, textured fabric, but does not get in the way of tailoring. The stockinette edges enhance the woven appearance of the fabric. The vertical lines of the buttons and edging elongate the jacket, giving it an elegant appearance.

Women's L: DALE OF NORWAY
Heilo - 17 balls #5545 Blue

Clarendon

Intermediate

STANDARD FIT

Finished measurements

Women's S (M, L)
A 39½ (42, 44½)"
B 20½ (22½, 25½)"
C 28½ (29½, 31¾)"

10cm/4"

32 / 24

over Twill pattern

1 2 **3** 4 5 6

Light weight
1600 (1850, 2100) yds

Eight 1" buttons

3.25mm/US 3
or size to obtain gauge

4 mm/US F

NOTES:

1 See Techniques (page 96) for 3-needle bind-off, one-row buttonhole, and seam instructions. *2* Work edge sts in Garter st (k every row). All increases and decreases are done after the beginning edge st or before the ending edge st. *3* Slip all sts purlwise.

Twill pattern (multiple of 4 sts plus 2; includes edge sts)
Row 1 and all WS rows K1, p across; end k1.
Row 2 (RS) K1, *k2, slip 2 with yarn in front (sl2 wyif); repeat from*, end k1.
Row 4 K2, *sl2 wyif, k2; repeat from*.
Row 6 K1, *sl2 wyif, k2; repeat from*, end k3.
Row 8 K1, sl1 wyif, *k2, sl2 wyif; repeat from*, end k2, sl1 wyif, k1.

Border pattern
Rows 1 and 3 (WS) K1, p across, end k1.
Row 2 and 4 K.
Row 5 K (fold line).
Row 6 and 8 K.
Row 7 K1, p across, k1.

BACK

Cast on 122 (126, 134) sts. Work 8 rows in Border pattern. Work in Twill pattern until Back measures 13 (14, 16)" from fold line, ending with a WS row.

Shape armholes

Bind off 9 sts at beginning of next 2 rows. Decrease 1 st each end of every RS row 9 times—86 (90, 98) sts remain. Work even until armhole measures 7 (8, 9)", ending with a WS row. Place all sts on hold.

LEFT FRONT

Cast on 82 (86, 90) sts. Work 8 rows in Border pattern. Work Twill pattern until Left Front matches Back length to underarm, ending with a WS row.

Shape armhole

Bind off 9 sts at beginning of next row (armhole edge). Work 1 row even. Decrease 1 st at armhole edge every RS row 9 times—64 (68, 72) sts. Work even until Left Front measures 17 (18, 21)", ending with a RS row.

Shape neck

Next row (WS) Bind off 28 (30, 32) sts (neck edge), and work to end of row. Work 1 row even. *Next row* Bind off 3 sts and work to end of row. Decrease 1 st at neck edge every RS rows 5 times—28 (30, 32) sts. Work even until armhole measures 8 (9, 10)", ending with a WS row. Place all sts on hold.

Place buttons

Mark placement of 2 rows of buttons on Left Front, the first 1" in from center edge, with the top of one button 1" below top neck edge, and 5" between remaining buttons. Mark the 2nd vertical row of buttons, approximately 4" to the right of the first row.

RIGHT FRONT

Work as for Left Front to mark for first pair of buttonholes.

Buttonholes

Next row (RS) Make one-row buttonholes as follows: work in pattern, work 6 sts, work first buttonhole

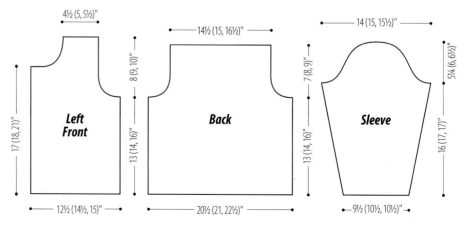

Left Front · 4½ (5, 5½)" · 17 (18, 21)" · 8 (9, 10)" · 13 (14, 16)" · 12½ (14½, 15)"

Back · 14½ (15, 16½)" · 13 (14, 16)" · 20½ (21, 22½)"

Sleeve · 14 (15, 15½)" · 5¼ (6, 6½)" · 7 (8, 9)" · 16 (17, 17)" · 9½ (10½, 10½)"

over 5 sts, work 18 sts in pattern, work 2nd buttonhole over 5 sts, work to end of row. Work even, repeating buttonholes where indicated on Left Front, **AT SAME TIME**, when Right Front matches Back length to underarm, shape armhole.

Shape armhole
Next row (WS) Bind off 9 sts at beginning of next WS row (armhole edge). Decrease 1 st at armhole edge every RS row 9 times—64 (68, 72) sts. Work even until Right Front matches Left Front length to neck, ending with a WS row.

Shape neck
Next row (RS) Bind off 28 (30, 32) sts, work to end of row. Work 1 row even. Bind off 3 sts at beginning of next RS row, work to end of row. Decrease 1 st at neck edge every RS rows 5 times—28 (30, 32) sts. Work even until armhole measures 8 (9, 10)", ending with a WS row. Place all sts on hold.

SLEEVES
Cast on 58 (62, 62) sts. Work 8 rows in Border pattern. Change to Twill pattern and increase 1 st at beginning and end of next RS row. Repeat this increase every 1 (1, ¾)", 12 (13, 15) more times—84 (90, 94) sts. Work even until Sleeve measures 16 (17, 17)" from fold line, ending with a WS row.

Shape cap
Bind off 9 sts at beginning of next 2 rows. Decrease 1 st at beginning and end of every RS row until 24 sts remain. Bind off.

ASSEMBLY
Shoulders
With RS together, join Front and Back shoulder seams by binding off the 28 (30, 32) sts of one shoulder in 3-needle bind-off; bind off 30 (30, 34) back neck stitches; then bind off remaining 28 (30, 32) sts in 3-needle bind-off.

Neck edge
On RS pick up and k 60 (64, 64) sts for Right Front neck, 30 (30, 34) sts for neck back, and 60 (64, 64) sts for Left Front neck—150 (158, 162) sts. Work Border pattern for 8 rows. Bind off.

Seams
With crochet slip st, set in sleeves, centering sleeve cap ½" forward from shoulder seam. Fold all borders toward inside at fold line and sew in place. With crochet slip st, join sleeve and side seams.

Front edge
With RS facing, pick up and k approximately 112 (118, 124) sts along each Front edge. Work Border pattern. Bind off, fold in half, and sew in place. Block garment. Sew on buttons.

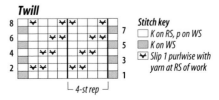

Twill

Stitch key
- ☐ K on RS, p on WS
- ▨ K on WS
- ⊻ Slip 1 purlwise with yarn at RS of work

└ 4-st rep ┘

Gloucester 17

This Chanel-style jacket was inspired by a wonderful fabric stitch that is particularly spectacular when worked in tweed yarn. I wanted this jacket to express the essence of a Chanel jacket: it has a V-neck, pockets, and a slit at the bottom of each sleeve, all accented with a crocheted two-toned braid.

Women's M: TAHKI
Donegal Tweed Homespun - MC 7 skeins #0884
Chelsea Silk - CC 1 skein each #118 and #122

Gloucester

Intermediate

STANDARD FIT

FINISHED measurements

Women's S (M, L, XL)
A 42 (45, 49, 53½)"
B 18½ (19½, 21½, 23½)"
C 27½ (29¼, 30¾, 31¼)"

10cm/4"

22 | GET GAUGE!
22

over Tweed pattern

1 2 3 **4** 5 6

Medium weight
Main color (MC)
1000 (1100, 1350, 1500) yds
   Color A
   100 yds
   Color B
   100 yds

Nine ¾" buttons

4.5 mm/US 7
or size to
obtain gauge

4 mm/US F

NOTES

1 See Techniques (page 96) for 3-needle bind-off, long-tail cast-on, ssk, buttonhole placement, and seam instructions. *2* Work edge sts in Garter st (k every row). All increases and decreases are worked after the beginning edge st or before the ending edge st. *3* Slip all sts purlwise.

Tweed pattern (multiple of 2; includes edge sts)

Row 1 (RS) K2, *sl1, k1, yo, pass sl st over both k1 and yo; repeat from*, end k2.
Row 2 K1, *p1 in 2nd st without removing st from left-hand needle, then p in first st. Slip both sts from left-hand needle; repeat from*, end k1.
Row 3 K.
Row 4 K1, p to last st, k1.

Crochet Braid

Round 1 With A, work 1 sc in first st on edge, *work 1 sc ½" into the Tweed pattern below the next st, 3 sc; repeat from* end sc 1. Join and ch 1.
Rounds 2 and 3 With B, sc in each stitch.
Round 4 With A, sc in each stitch.

BACK

With MC, cast on 118 (124, 136, 144) sts. P 1 row (WS). Work in Tweed pattern until Back measures 11 (12, 13, 14)", ending with a WS row.

Shape armholes

Bind off 10 sts at beginning of next 2 rows. Decrease 1 st at beginning and end of every RS row 8 (8, 11, 12) times—82 (88, 94, 100) sts. Work even until armhole

measures approximately 7 (7, 8, 9)", ending with row 4. Place all sts on hold.

LEFT FRONT

With MC, cast on 58 (64, 70, 76) sts. P 1 row (WS). Work in Tweed pattern until Left Front matches Back length to underarm, ending with a WS row.

Shape armhole and neck

Bind off 10 sts at beginning of row (armhole edge), work to 3 sts remaining and k2tog, k1 (neck edge). Work 1 row even. Decrease 1 st at armhole edge every RS row 8 (8, 11, 12) times, **AT SAME TIME**, decrease 1 st at neck edge every RS row 15 (18, 19, 21) more times—24 (27, 29, 32) sts. Work even until armhole measures approximately 8 (8, 9, 10)", ending with row 4. Place all sts on hold.

RIGHT FRONT

With MC, cast on 58 (64, 70, 76) sts. P 1 row (WS). Work in Tweed pattern until Right Front matches Back length to underarm, ending with a RS row.

Shape armhole and neck

Bind off 10 sts at beginning of row (armhole edge), work to end of row. *Next row* (RS) K1, ssk (neck edge), work to 2 sts remaining and decrease 1 (armhole edge). On every RS row, decrease 1 st at armhole edge every RS row 7 (7, 10, 11) more times, **AT SAME TIME**, decrease 1 st at neck edge every RS row 15 (18, 19, 21) more times—24 (27, 29, 32) sts. Work even until Front armhole measures approximately 8 (8, 9, 10)", ending with row 4. Place all sts on hold.

POCKETS (Make 2)

With MC, cast on 28 sts. P 1 row (WS). Work 3½" in Tweed pattern, ending with row 4. Bind off.

SLEEVES

Cuffs (Make 2)

With MC, cast on 26 sts. P 1 row (WS). Work 2½" in Tweed pattern, ending with row 2. Place all sts on hold. Repeat from *to* leaving work on needle. *Next row* (RS) Work in pat across row, then work sts from hold—52 sts. Work 1 row even.

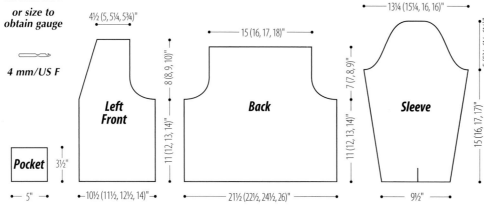

4½ (5, 5¼, 5¾)"

13¼ (15¼, 16, 16)"

15 (16, 17, 18)"

8 (8, 9, 10)"

7 (7, 8, 9)"

5 (5¾, 6¼, 6¾)"

Left Front

11 (12, 13, 14)"

Back

11 (12, 13, 14)"

Sleeve

15 (16, 17, 17)"

Pocket

3½"

5"

10½ (11½, 12½, 14)"

21½ (22½, 24½, 26)"

9½"

Increase 1 sts at beginning and end of next RS row and repeat increases every 6(4, 4, 4)th row, 11 (15, 17, 17) more times—76 (84, 88, 88) sts. Work even until sleeve measures 14 (14½, 15, 15)", ending with row 2.

Shape cap

Bind off 10 sts at beginning of next 2 rows. Decrease 1 st at beginning and end of every RS row until 38 (44, 44, 44) sts remain. Then decrease 1 st at beginning and end of every row until 18 (20, 22, 22) sts remain. Bind off.

ASSEMBLY
Shoulders

With RS together and using MC, join Front and Back shoulder seams by binding off the 24 (27, 29, 32) sts of one shoulder in 3-needle bind-off; bind off 34 (34, 36, 36) back neck stitches; then bind off remaining 24 (27, 29, 32) sts in 3-needle bind-off.

Seams

With crochet slip stitch and MC, set in sleeves, centering sleeve cap ½" forward from shoulder seam; then join sleeve and side seams.

Mark for buttonholes

On Left Front, mark placement of buttons: the top of one just below start of V-neck shaping, and the bottom of one 3" from bottom, with the remaining 3 placed evenly between. Sew on buttons. On Right Front, mark placement of buttonholes to match.

CROCHET BRAID TRIM
Pockets

Work Crochet Braid across top of pockets, **EXCEPT** work in rows. Do not join; at the end of each row, chain 1 and turn. Center pockets on each Front about 1" above bottom edge and sew in place.

Body

Starting at Right Front side seam, with RS facing, work Round 1 of Crochet Braid around all edges, working 2 sts at front bottom corners and start of V-neck shaping. Work Rounds 2 to 4 of braid, continuing to work 1 additional st at turning points as worked in Round 1. **AT SAME TIME**, on Round 2, work to buttonhole markers, and chain 3, skip 3 sts, and sc in 4th st. *Next round* Work 3 sc in the chain-3 loop.

Right cuff

With RS facing, work Round 1 of Crochet Braid starting at top right side of cuff vent and working to bottom edge of left side. Work rounds 2 to 4 of braid, making 2 buttonholes as for body, placed ½" above bottom edge of vent, and the 2nd 1" above the 1st.

Left cuff

Work as for Right Sleeve, starting trim at bottom edge of right side of vent, and working to top edge of left side of vent, placing buttonholes as on Right Sleeve. Sew braid at top of vent down over opposite side of vent. Sew on buttons. Block garment.

Hanover 18

The quilted cotton jackets I've seen in specialty shops inspired this jacket. These jackets often have outlined flowers and leaves atop the quilted background. I used ribbing and a leaf medallion to mimic the effect. I centered the leaf pattern on the bottom of the back and front panels and on each cuff. The transition from leaf to rib is effortless.

Women's M: DALESPUN
Heilo - 13 balls #6545 Teal Blue

Hanover

STANDARD FIT

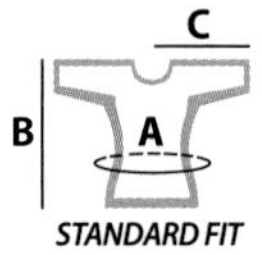

FINISHED measurements

Women's S (M, L)
A 39¾ (43¾, 47¾)"
B 19½ (21½, 22½)"
C 28½ (29¼, 30½)"

10cm/4"

32 GET GAUGE!

24

over Shadow rib

1 2 **3** 4 5 6

Light weight
1600 (1700, 2100) yds

3.5 mm/US 4 - 24" circular
or size to obtain gauge

4 mm/US F

NOTES

1 See Techniques (page 96) for 3-needle bind-off, lifted increase, one-row buttonhole, ssk, SK2P, and seam instructions. *2* Work edge sts in Garter st (k every row). All increases and decreases are done after the beginning edge st or before the ending edge st. *3* Slip all sts purlwise.

Shadow rib (multiple of 3 sts plus 1; includes edge sts)
Row 1 (RS) K.
Row 2 K1, *p2, k next st in back loop (k1b); repeat from*, end p2, k1.

Leaf Medallion (begins with 22 sts, ends with 1 st)
Reverse decrease (rev dec) Ssk; slip stitch remaining from ssk to left needle, pass second stitch on left needle over ssk and off needle, slip ssk to right needle.
Row 1 (RS) K6, rev dec, yo, k1, yo, p2, yo, k1, yo, SK2P, k6.
Rows 2, 4, 6, 8 P10, k2, p10.
Row 3 K4, rev dec, k1, (yo, k1) 2 times, p2, k1, (yo, k1) 2 times, SK2P, k4.
Row 5 K2, rev dec, k2, yo, k1, yo, k2, p2, k2, yo, k1, yo, k2, SK2P, k2.
Row 7 Rev dec, k3, yo, k1, yo, k3, p2, k3, yo, k1, yo, k3, SK2P.
Rows 9–15 Repeat Rows 1–7.
Row 16 P10, k2tog, p10—21 sts.
Note On RS rows 17–33 the leaf is shaped by the first and last decreases in each row. Stitch count is maintained by lifted increases on either side of the leaf. Increased stitches are worked in Shadow rib on following rows. The leaf ends in one stitch on row 35.

Beginning with the next row, all stitches are worked in Shadow rib pattern.
Row 17 Lifted increase (M1), ssk, k6 , k2tog, yo, k1, yo, ssk, k6, k2tog, M1.
WS rows 18–34 Purl all leaf sts.
Row 19 M1, ssk, k4, k2tog, (k1, yo) 2 times, k1, ssk, k4, k2tog, M1.
Row 21 M1, ssk, k2, k2tog, k2, yo, k1, yo, k2, ssk, k2, k2tog, M1.
Row 23 M1, ssk, k2tog, k3, yo, k1, yo, k3, ssk, k2tog, M1.
Row 25 M1, k2tog, k9, ssk, M1.
Row 27 M1, ssk, k7, k2tog, M1.
Row 29 M1, ssk, k5, k2tog, M1.
Row 31 M1, ssk, k3, k2tog, M1.
Row 33 M1, ssk, k1, k2tog, M1.
Row 35 SK2P, M1.

BACK

Cast on 120 (132, 144) sts. K 1 row (WS). *Next row* (RS) K49 (55, 61), place marker (pm), work 22 sts in Leaf Medallion pattern, pm, k to end. *Next row* (WS) Working row 2 of patterns, work Shadow rib to first marker, Leaf Medallion to second marker, Shadow rib (beginning with k1b) to end. Work in patterns as established until Leaf Medallion is completed—118 (130, 142) sts, then in Shadow rib for all sts, until Back measures 12 (13, 14)", ending with a WS row.
Shape armholes
Bind off 10 sts at beginning of next 2 rows. Decrease 1 st at beginning and end of every RS row 8 (10, 12) times—82 (90, 98) sts. Work even until armhole measures 7 (8, 8)", ending with a WS row. Place all sts on hold.

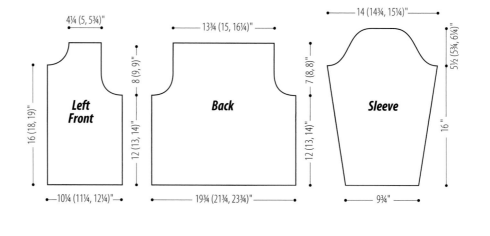

4¼ (5, 5¾)"

8 (9, 9)"

16 (18, 19)"

12 (13, 14)"

Left Front

10¼ (11¼, 12¼)"

13¾ (15, 16¼)"

Back

7 (8, 8)"

12 (13, 14)"

19¾ (21¾, 23¾)"

14 (14¾, 15¼)"

5½ (5¾, 6¼)"

Sleeve

16"

9¾"

LEFT FRONT

Cast on 63 (69, 75) sts. K 1 row (WS). *Next row* (RS) K19 (22, 25), place marker (pm), work 22 sts in Leaf Medallion pattern, pm, k to end. *Next row* (WS) Working row 2 of patterns, work Shadow rib to first marker, Leaf Medallion to second marker, Shadow rib (beginning with k1b) to end. Work in patterns as established until Leaf Medallion is completed—61 (67, 73) sts, then in Shadow rib for all sts until Left Front matches Back length to underarm, ending with a WS row.

Shape armhole

Bind off 10 sts (armhole edge) and work to end of row. Work 1 row even. *Next row* (RS) Decrease 1 st at armhole edge every RS row 8 (10, 12) times—43 (47, 51) sts. Work even in pattern until Front measures 16 (18, 19)", ending with a RS row.

Shape neck

Next row (WS) Bind off 10 sts (neck edge) and work to end of row. Decrease 1 st at neck edge every RS row 7 times—26 (30, 34) sts. Work even until armhole measures 8 (9, 9)", ending with a WS row. Place all sts on hold.

RIGHT FRONT

Cast on 63 (69, 75) sts. K 1 row (WS). *Next row* (RS) K22 (25, 28), place marker (pm), work 22 sts in Leaf Medallion pattern, pm, k to end. *Next row* (WS) Working row 2 of patterns, work Shadow rib to first marker, Leaf Medallion to second marker, Shadow rib (beginning with k1b) to end. Work in patterns as established until Leaf Medallion is completed—61 (67, 73) sts, then Shadow rib for all sts until Right Front matches Back length to underarm, ending with a RS row.

Shape armhole

Bind off 10 sts (armhole edge) and work to end of row. *Next row* (RS) Decrease 1 st at armhole edge every RS row 8 (10, 12) times—43 (47, 51) sts. Work even in pattern until Front measures 16 (18, 19)", ending with a WS row.

Shape neck

Next row (RS) Bind off 10 sts (neck edge) and work to end of row. Work 1 row even. Decrease 1 st at neck edge every RS row 7 times—26 (30, 34) sts. Work even until armhole measures 8 (9, 9)", ending with a WS row. Place all sts on hold.

SLEEVES

Cast on 60 sts. K 1 row. *Next row* (RS) K19, place marker (pm), work 22 sts in Leaf Medallion pattern, pm, k to end. *Next row* (WS) Working row 2 of patterns, work Shadow rib to first marker, Leaf Medallion to second marker, Shadow rib (beginning with k1b) to end. Work in patterns as established for 1", ending with a WS row. Increase 1 sts at beginning and end of next row. Repeat increase every 1" 12 (14, 16) more times—84 (88, 92) sts. Work even in pattern until Sleeve measures 16", ending with a WS row.

Shape cap

Bind off 10 sts at beginning of next 2 rows. Decrease 1 st at beginning and end of every RS row until 20 (22, 22) sts remain. Bind off.

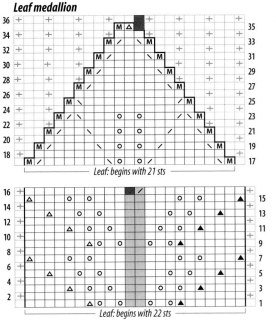

Leaf medallion

Leaf: begins with 21 sts

Leaf: begins with 22 sts

Shadow rib

3-st rep

Stitch key

☐ K on RS, p on WS
▨ P on RS, k on WS
☑ P2tog
◩ Ssk
◪ K2tog
△ SK2P
▲ Reverse decrease
○ Yo
M Lifted increase
+ K1b
■ Skip to next square

Grayed areas show how Leaf Medallion fits into Shadow rib pattern.

Hanover

ASSEMBLY
Shoulders
With RS together, join Front and Back shoulder seams by binding off the 26 (30, 34) sts of one shoulder in 3-needle bind-off; bind off 30 back neck stitches; then bind off remaining 26 (30, 34) sts in 3-needle bind-off.

Neck and front edging
With RS facing, skip first 6 sts at Right Front edge, pick up 72 (80, 88) sts around neck ending 6 sts from Left Front edge. Work 4 repeats of Shadow rib pattern. Place all sts on hold. With circular needle pick up 96 (108, 114) sts on Right Front edge, 6 sts on neck edge, 6 sts on side of collar, k collar sts from hold, pick up 6 sts on side of collar, 6 sts on neck edge, and 96 (108, 114) sts on the Left Front edge—288 (320, 340) sts. K 1 row. Bind off.

Seams
With crochet slip st, set in sleeves, centering sleeve cap ½" forward from shoulder seam, then join sleeve and side seams.
Block garment.

Siobhan 19

Linen yarn first says to me lace, lace, lace. This emerald green reminded me of lush green leaves, so the combination meant a leaf—a lacy leaf. The leaf pattern I used in this jacket is easy to modify, which provided me the opportunity to shape a peplum with lace columns that evolve into smaller repeating leaf shapes. The jacket is especially suitable for summer evening wear.

Women's M: LOUET
Euroflax Sportweight - 5 skeins Emerald

Siobhan

STANDARD FIT

FINISHED measurements

Women's XS (S, M, L)
A 32½ (38, 43, 48½)"
B 23 (25½, 25½, 28)"
C 25¾ (29¾, 31½, 33)"

10cm/4"

over Leaf pattern,
4" is 3 repeats wide

Light weight
1200 (1400, 1600, 1800) yds

One 1" button

3.25 mm/US 3
or size to obtain gauge

4 mm/US F

NOTES

1 See Techniques (page 96) for 3-needle bind-off, ssk, one-row buttonhole, crab st, and seam instructions. *2* Work edge st in Garter st (k every row). All increases and decreases are worked after the beginning edge st or before the ending edge st. *3* The Peplum is shaped by decreases built into the pattern in rows 25 and 41. *4* The stitch count changes within the Leaf pattern: there is one more stitch on rows 5–20. Be aware of this as you maintain the pattern through garment's shaping.

Peplum (starts with multiple of 13 sts; includes edge sts)
Row 1 (RS) K1, *k5, yo, ssk, yo, k4, ssk; repeat from*, end k1.
Rows 2 and 4 K1, p across, end k1.
Row 3 K1, *k2tog, k4, yo, k1, yo, k4, ssk; repeat from*, end k1.
Rows 5–24 Repeat rows 3 and 4 ten more times.
Row 25 (Decrease row) K1, *k2tog, k2, k2tog, yo, k1, yo, ssk, k2, ssk; repeat from*, end k1—2 sts decreased on each repeat of pattern.
Rows 26 and 28 K1, p across, end k1.
Row 27 K1, *k2tog, k3, yo, k1, yo, k3, ssk; repeat from*, end k1.
Rows 29–40 Repeat rows 27 and 28 six more times.
Row 41 (Decrease row) K1, *k2 tog, k1, k2tog, yo, k1, yo, ssk, k1, ssk; repeat from*, end k1—2 sts decreased on each repeat of pattern.
Rows 42 and 44 K1, p across, end k1.
Row 43 K1, *k2tog, k2, yo, k1, yo, k2, ssk; repeat from*, end k1.
Rows 45–52 Repeat rows 43 and 44 four more times.

Leaf pattern (starts and ends with multiple of 9 plus 2; includes edge sts)
Row 1 (RS) K1, *k2tog, k1, yo, k3, yo, k1, ssk; repeat from*, end k1.
Row 2 and all WS rows K1, p across, end k1.
Row 3 K1, *k2tog, yo, k5, yo, ssk; repeat from*, end k1.
Row 5 K2, *yo, k2, ssk, k3, yo, ssk, repeat from*, end last repeat k2—1 st increased.
Row 7 K2, *yo, k2, ssk, k2tog, k2, yo, k1; repeat from*, end k1.
Rows 9–16 Repeat rows 7 and 8 four more times.
Row 17 K3, *yo, k1, ssk, k2tog, k1, yo, k3; repeat from*.
Row 19 K4,*yo, ssk, k2tog, yo, k5; repeat from*, end last repeat k4.
Row 21 K1, k2tog, k2, *yo, ssk, yo, k2, ssk, k3; repeat from*, end last repeat k1—1 st decreased, back to original number of sts.
Row 23 K1, *k2tog, k2, yo, k1, yo, k2, ssk; repeat from*, end k1.
Rows 25–32 Repeat rows 23 and 24 four more times. Repeat these 32 rows for pattern.

Cuff pattern (multiple of 9 plus 2; includes edge sts)
Row 1 K1, *k3, yo, ssk, yo, k2, ssk; repeat from*, end k1.
Rows 2 and 4 K1, p across, end k1.
Row 3 K1, *k2tog, k2, yo, k1, yo, k2, ssk; repeat from*, end k1.
Rows 5–24 Repeat rows 3 and 4 ten more times.

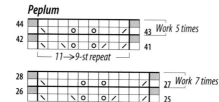

Peplum

44 ... 43 Work 5 times
42 ... 41
└─ 11→9-st repeat ─┘

28 ... 27 Work 7 times
26 ... 25
└─ 13→11-st repeat ─┘

4 ... 3 Work 11 times
2 ... 1
└─ 13-st repeat ─┘

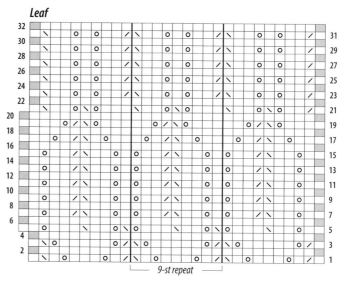

Leaf

└─ 9-st repeat ─┘

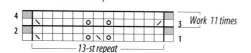

BACK

Cast on 158 (184, 210, 236) sts. K 1 row. *Next row* (RS) Work Peplum pattern rows 1–52, decreasing to 134 (156, 178, 200) sts on Row 25 and to 110 (128, 146, 164) sts on Row 41. Peplum should measure approximately 8". Change to Leaf pattern and work even until Back measures 15½ (17½, 17½, 19)", ending with a WS row.

Shape armholes

Next row (RS) Bind off 9 sts at beginning of next 2 rows. Decrease 1 st at beginning and end of every RS row 9 times—74 (92, 110, 128) sts. Work even in pattern until armhole measures approximately 7½ (8, 8, 9)", ending with row 16 or 32 of Leaf pattern. Place all sts on hold.

LEFT FRONT

Cast on 80 (93, 106, 119) sts. K 1 row (WS). *Next row* (RS) Work Peplum rows 1–52, decreasing to 68 (79, 90, 101) sts on Row 25 and to 56 (65, 74, 83) sts on Row 41. Change to Leaf pattern and work until Left Front matches Back length to underarm, ending with a WS row.

Shape armhole

Next row (RS) Bind off 9 sts at beginning of row, work to end of row. Work 1 row even. Decrease 1 st at beginning of every RS row 9 times—38 (47, 56, 65) sts. Work even until Left Front measures approximately 20½ (23, 23, 25½)", ending with row 15 or 31 of Leaf pattern.

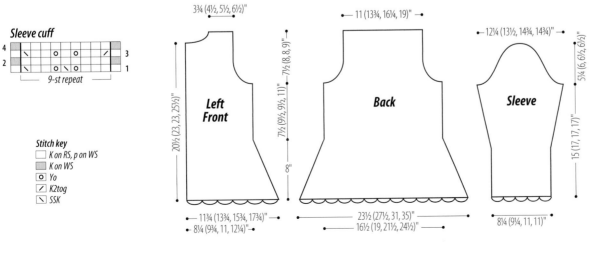

Sleeve cuff

4
2
3
1

9-st repeat

Stitch key

☐ K on RS, p on WS
▨ K on WS
◉ Yo
⟋ K2tog
⟍ SSK

3¾ (4½, 5½, 6½)"

11 (13¾, 16¼, 19)"

12¼ (13½, 14¾, 14¾)"

Left Front

20½ (23, 23, 25½)"

7½ (9½, 9½, 11)"

7½ (8, 8, 9)"

8"

11¾ (13¾, 15¾, 17¾)"

8¼ (9¾, 11, 12¼)"

Back

23½ (27½, 31, 35)"

16½ (19, 21½, 24½)"

Sleeve

5¼ (6, 6½, 6½)"

15 (17, 17, 17)"

8¼ (9¼, 11, 11)"

Siobhan

Shape neck
Next row (WS) Bind off 8 (10, 12, 14) sts, work to end of row. *Next row* (RS) Decrease 1 st at neck edge every RS row 6 (7, 8, 9) times—24 (30, 36, 42) sts. Work even until Left Front length matches Back, ending with a WS row. Place all sts on hold.

RIGHT FRONT
Work same as Left Front to underarm, **EXCEPT** end with a RS row.

Shape armhole
Next row (WS) Bind off 9 sts at beginning of row, work to end of row. Decrease 1 st at beginning of every RS row 9 times—38 (47, 56, 65) sts. Work even until Left Front measures approximately 20½ (23, 23, 25½)", ending with row 15 or 31 of Leaf pattern.

Shape neck
Next row (RS) Bind off 8 (10, 12, 14) sts, work to end of row. *Next row* (WS) Decrease 1 st at neck edge every RS row 6 (7, 8, 9) times—24 (30, 36, 42) sts. Work even until Left Front length matches Back, ending with a WS row. Place all sts on hold.

SLEEVES
Cast on 56 (65, 74, 74) sts. Work Cuff pattern rows 1–24. Change to Leaf pattern and increase 1 st at beginning and end of next row (working increases into pattern), then every 4th row 12 more times—82 (91, 100, 100) sts. Work even until Sleeve measures 15 (17, 17, 17)".

Shape cap
Bind off 9 sts at beginning of next 2 rows. Decrease 1 st at beginning and end of every RS row 10 (12, 13, 13) times. Work 1 row even. *Next row* (RS) Decrease 1 st at beginning and end of every row 13 (14, 15, 16) times—18 (21, 26, 24) sts. Bind off.

ASSEMBLY
Shoulders
With RS together, join Front and Back shoulder seams by binding off the 24 (30, 36, 42) sts of one shoulder in 3-needle bind-off; bind off 26 (32, 38, 44) back neck sts; then bind off remaining 24 (30, 36, 42) sts in 3-needle bind-off.

Neck edge
With RS facing, pick up and k 28 sts on right neck edge, 26 (32, 38, 44) on back neck, and 28 on left neck edge—82 (88, 94, 100) sts. Work 8 rows of Garter stitch (4 ridges). Bind off.

Front edge
Pick up 110 (120, 120, 130) sts along Left Front edge. Work 8 rows of Garter stitch. Bind off. Measure 9" from neck edge and mark for button. Mark buttonhole placement on Right Front to match. Work Right Front edge as for Left, **EXCEPT** make one-row buttonhole over 4 sts on 3rd row of Garter st edge at buttonhole marker.

Seams
With crochet slip st, set in sleeves, then join sleeve and side seams. Block garment. Sew on button.

83

Nashua20

This stitch pattern fascinated me. It's just a combination of knits and purls with the knit stitches being slipped every other row, yet it gives dimension to the fabric without adding a lot of bulk, and it's really simple to knit. The fabric is so interesting that I have kept the details simple: no collar, no pockets.

Women's M: LOUET
Merino Yarn, Sportweight - 8 skeins #57 French Blue

Nashua

NOTES

1 See Techniques (page 96) for 3-needle bind-off, buttonhole placement, double yo, and seam instructions. *2* Work edge sts in Garter st (k every row). All increases and decreases are worked after the beginning edge st or before the ending edge st. *3* Slip all sts purlwise.

Seersucker pattern (multiple of 12 plus 3; includes edge sts)

Row 1 (RS) K1, p5, *k3, p9; repeat from*, end k3, p5, k1.
Row 2 K6, *slip 3 purlwise with yarn in front (sl3 wyif), k9; repeat from*, end sl3 wyif, k6.

BACK

Cast on 123 (135, 147) sts. Work 6 rows of garter st (k every row). P1 row (WS). Work in Seersucker pattern until Back measures 7 (8, 8)", ending with a WS row.

Shape armholes

Bind off 10 sts at beginning of next 2 rows, then decrease 1 st at beginning and end of every RS row 7 times—89 (101, 113) sts. Work even until armhole measures 7 (8, 8)". Place all sts on hold.

LEFT FRONT

Cast on 58 (70, 82) sts. Work 6 rows of garter st. P1 row (WS). Work in Seersucker pattern until Left Front matches Back length to underarm, ending with a WS row.

Shape armhole

Next row (RS) Bind off 10 sts (armhole edge) and work to end. Decrease 1 st at armhole edge every RS row 7 times—41 (53, 65) sts. Work even until Left Front measures 17 (19, 20)", ending with a RS row.

Shape neck

Next row (WS) Bind off 10 (13, 16) sts (neck edge), work to end of row. Work 1 row even. *Next row* Bind off 3 sts, work to end of row. Decrease 1 st at neck edge every RS row 4 (8, 11) times—24 (29, 35) sts remaining. Work even until armhole measures 8 (9, 9)", ending with a WS row. Place all sts on hold.

RIGHT FRONT

Work to match Left Front to underarm, ending with a RS row.

Shape armhole

Next row Bind off 10 sts (armhole edge) and work to end. Decrease 1 st at armhole edge every RS row 7 times—41 (53, 65) sts. Work even until Front measures 17 (19, 20)", ending with a WS row.

Shape neck

Next row (RS) Bind off 10 (13, 16) sts (neck edge), work to end of row. Work 1 row even. *Next row* Bind off 3 sts, work to end of row. Decrease 1 st at neck edge every RS row 4 (8, 11) times—24 (29, 35) sts remaining. Work even until armhole measures 8 (9, 9)", ending with WS row. Place all sts on hold.

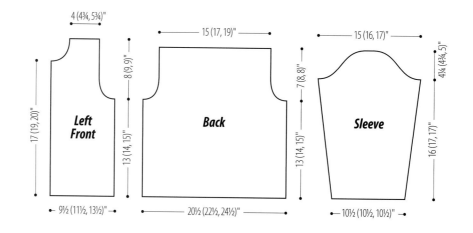

Left Front
4 (4¾, 5¾)"
8 (9, 9)"
17 (19, 20)"
13 (14, 15)"
9½ (11½, 13½)"

Back
15 (17, 19)"
7 (8, 8)"
13 (14, 15)"
20½ (22½, 24½)"

Sleeve
15 (16, 17)"
4¼ (4¾, 5)"
16 (17, 17)"
10½ (10½, 10½)"

SLEEVES

Cast on 63 sts. Work 6 rows of Garter st. P 1 row (WS).
Work in Seersucker pattern until Sleeve measures 1".
Increase 1 st at beginning and end of next RS row.
Repeat increases every 1 (¾, ¾)" 13 (16, 19) times
more—91 (97, 103) sts. Work even until Sleeve
measures 16 (17, 17)", ending with a WS row.

Shape cap

Bind off 10 sts at beginning of next 2 rows. Decrease
1 st at beginning and end of every RS row to 21 (21,
23) sts. Bind off.

ASSEMBLY

Shoulders

With RS together, join Front and Back shoulder seams
by binding off the 24 (29, 35) sts of one shoulder
in 3-needle bind-off; bind off 41 (43, 43) back neck
stitches; then bind off remaining 24 (29, 35) sts in 3-
needle bind-off.

Neck edging

With RS facing, pick up approximately 96 (102, 108) sts
at neck edge. Work 6 rows of Garter st. Bind off.

Left front edging

With RS of Left Front facing, pick up and k
approximately 100 (108, 116) sts along center Front
edge. Work 6 rows of Garter st. Bind off. Mark
placement of 6 buttons: the top of one ½" from top
and the bottom of one 1" from bottom, with the other
4 placed evenly between. Sew on buttons.

Right front edging

Mark placement of buttonholes to match the buttons.
With RS facing, pick up and k sts as worked on Left
Front for 2 rows. *Next row*, k as for left side, **EXCEPT**
when you reach markers for buttonholes, k2tog,
double yo. Work to end of row. Work 3 more rows of
Garter st. Bind off.

Seams

With crochet slip st, set in sleeves, centering sleeve
cap ½" forward from the shoulder seam, then join
sleeve and side seams. Block garment.

Seersucker

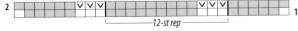

2 ———— 12-st rep ———— 1

Stitch key
☐ K on RS
▨ P on RS, k on WS
☑ Slip 1 purlwise with
   yarn at WS of work

Arlington 21

A tailored, well-fitting jacket can take you wherever you want to go. This navy blazer, with your choice of three collars, is just too sophisticated to stay home after work. Metallic thread, sequins, and crystals light up the night.

Women's M: DALE OF NORWAY
Tiur - 15 balls #5664 Navy

Arlington

Advanced

STANDARD FIT

FINISHED measurements
Women's S (M, L, XL, XXL)
A 39¼ (42½, 45½, 49, 52¼)"
B 21½ (23½, 24½, 24½, 25½)"
C 28¼ (30¼, 31¼, 31¼, 31¾)"

10cm/4"

48
25
GET GAUGE!

over Slip stitch pattern

1 2 **3** 4 5 6

Light weight
1700 (1900, 2100) yds

Eighteen ¾" buttons

3.5 mm/US 4
or size to obtain gauge

4mm/US F

&

Five hooks and eyes
Leaf Collar
Metallic blending filament
100 yds
Sequin Collar
Sequins ¾" (19mm)–
306 (318, 330, 342, 366)
Cobweb Collar
Crystal beads–67 (70, 72, 76, 83)

NOTE

1 See Techniques (page 96) for ssk, lifted increase, 3-needle bind-off, SK2P, and SP2P. **2** Slip sts purlwise with yarn at right side (RS) of work.

Slip st pattern
Rows 1 and 3 (RS) Knit.
Row 2 K1, *k1, sl 1; repeat from*, end k1.
Row 4 K1, *sl 1, k1; repeat from*, end k1.

BACK
Cast on 124 (134, 144, 154, 164) sts. [P 1 row, k 1 row] twice. K 1 row on WS (turning ridge). [K 1 row, p 1 row] twice. Work 1" in Slip st pattern, ending with a WS row.

Shape waist
Next row (RS) K29 (32, 34, 37, 39), ssk, place marker (pm), k2tog, k58 (62, 68, 72, 78), ssk, pm, k2tog, k to end of row. Repeat decrease row every 6th row 5 more times, working ssk before markers and k2tog after markers—100 (110, 120, 130, 140) sts. Work 2 (3, 3, 3, 3)" even, slipping markers every row, ending with a WS row. *Next row* (RS) *K to 1 st before marker, work lifted increase in next st, slip marker, work lifted increase in next st; repeat from* once more, k to end of row. Repeat increase row every 6th row 5 times more—124 (134, 144, 154, 164) sts. Work even (removing markers) until piece measures 14 (15, 16, 16, 16)" above turning ridge, ending with a WS row.

Shape armholes
Bind off 10 (10, 10, 12, 14) sts at beginning of next 2 rows. Decrease 1 st at beginning and end of every RS row 6 (6, 6, 7, 8) times—92 (102, 112, 116, 120) sts. Work even until armhole measures 7 (8, 8, 8, 9)". Place all sts on hold.

RIGHT FRONT
Cast on 62 (68, 72, 78, 82) sts. Work as for Back to waist shaping.

Shape waist
Next row (RS) K29 (32, 34, 37, 39), ssk, pm, k2tog, k to end of row. Repeat decrease row every 6th row 5 more times, working ssk before marker and k2tog after marker—50 (56, 60, 66, 70) sts. Work 2 (3, 3, 3, 3)" even, slipping marker every row, ending with a WS row. *Next row* (RS) K to 1 st before marker, work lifted increase in next st, slip marker, work lifted increase

in next st, k to end of row. Repeat increase row every 6th row 5 times more—62 (68, 72, 78, 82) sts. Work even until piece measures same length as Back to underarm, ending with a WS row.

Shape armhole and V-neck
Decrease 1 st at neck edge (beginning of RS rows) on next row, then every other row 11 (8, 10, 10, 4) times more, then every 4th row 7 (11, 11, 12, 18) times, **AT SAME TIME**, shape armhole at side edge as for Back—27 (32, 34, 36, 37) sts. Work even until armhole measures 8 (9, 9, 9, 10)," ending with a WS row. Place all sts on hold.

LEFT FRONT
Work as for Right Front, reversing armhole and neck shaping.

SLEEVES
Cast on 54 (58, 58, 62, 62) sts. [P1 row, k1 row] twice. K1 row on WS (turning ridge). [K1 row, p1 row] twice. Work 1" in Slip st pattern, end with WS row. Continue in pattern, increasing 1 st at beginning and end of RS row (working increases into pattern) on next row, then every 10 (10, 8, 8, 6) th row 4 (10, 9, 17, 9) more times, every 12 (12, 10, 10, 8) th row 10 (6, 10, 3, 14) times—84 (92, 98, 104, 110) sts. Work even until piece measures 16 (17, 17, 16½, 16½)" above turning ridge, ending with a WS row.

Shape cap
Bind off 10 (10, 10, 12, 14) sts at beginning of next 2 rows. Decrease 1 st at beginning and end of every RS row 28 (30, 32, 33, 34) times—8 (12, 14, 14, 14) sts. Work 1 row even. Bind off.

ASSEMBLY
Block pieces.
Shoulders
With RS together, join Front and Back shoulder seams by binding off the 27 (32, 34, 36,37) sts of one shoulder in 3-needle bind-off; bind off 38 (38, 44, 44, 46) back neck stitches; then bind off remaining 27 (32, 34, 36, 37) sts in 3-needle bind-off.
Seams
With crochet slip stitch, set in sleeves, centering sleeve cap ½" forward from shoulder seam; then slip st side

and sleeve seams. Fold borders at lower edges of body and sleeves to WS at turning ridge and sew in place.

Front and neck border

With RS facing and circular needle, begin at lower edge of Right Front and pick up and k78 (84, 90, 86, 86) sts to beginning of V-neck shaping, 48 (52, 52, 56, 62) sts to shoulder, 36 (36, 42, 42, 44) sts along back neck, 48 (52, 52, 56, 62) sts along Left Front V-neck, and 78 (84, 90, 86, 86) sts to lower edge—288 (308, 326, 326, 340) sts. Work 9 rows of border as for body. Bind off. Fold to WS at turning ridge and sew in place. Sew 5 buttons along Right Front edge on pick-up row of border, with the first button at beginning of V-neck shaping, the last approximately 2" above turning ridge, and 3 others spaced evenly between. Sew buttons on Left Front to correspond. Sew hooks onto WS of Right Front edge under buttons, and sew eyes on WS of Left Front. Sew on remaining 8 buttons as follows: sew 1 button ½" in front of right shoulder seam; 2 buttons evenly spaced between shoulder button and V-neck button, repeat on Left Front; 2 buttons on Back.

SEQUIN COLLAR

27 (28, 29, 30, 32)" long x 2½" wide

Cast on 153 (159, 165, 171, 183) sts. **Work Sequin pattern: *Rows 1 and 3*** (RS) K. ***Row 2*** (sequin row; WS) *K1, place sequin on next st (see illustration), k1; repeat from*. ***Row 4*** K. Repeat rows 1–4 four times

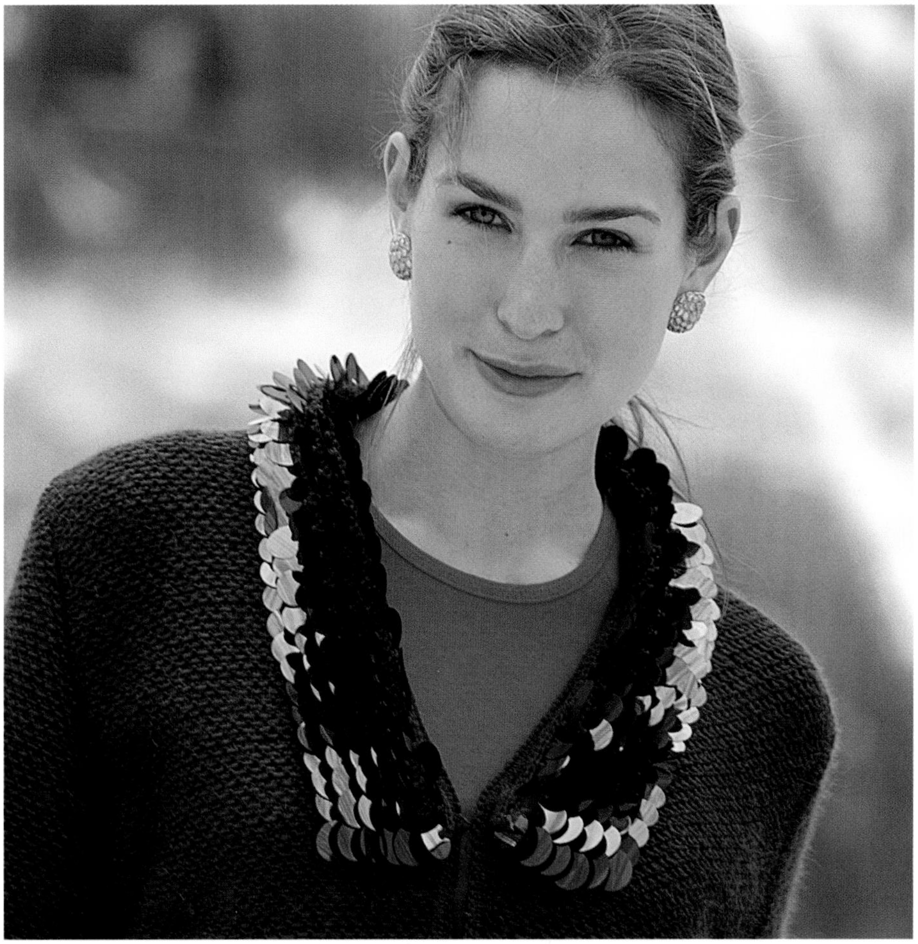

Knit-on sequin

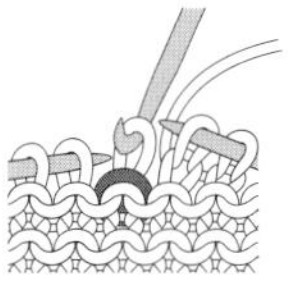

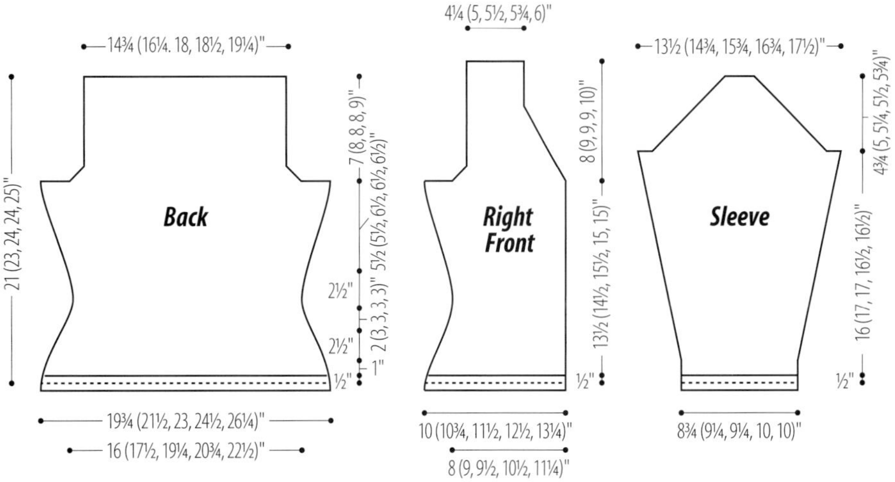

14¾ (16¼. 18, 18½, 19¼)"
21 (23, 24, 24, 25)"
7 (8, 8, 8, 9)"
5½ (5½, 6½, 6½, 6½)"
2 (3, 3, 3, 3)"
2½"
2½"
1"
½"
Back
19¾ (21½, 23, 24½, 26¼)"
16 (17½, 19¼, 20¾, 22½)"
4¼ (5, 5½, 5¾, 6)"
8 (9, 9, 9, 10)"
13½ (14½, 15½, 15, 15)"
½"
Right Front
10 (10¾, 11½, 12½, 13¼)"
8 (9, 9½, 10½, 11¼)"
13½ (14¾, 15¾, 16¾, 17½)"
4¾ (5, 5¼, 5½, 5¾)"
16 (17, 17, 16½, 16½)"
½"
Sleeve
8¾ (9¼, 9¼, 10, 10)"

Chart D

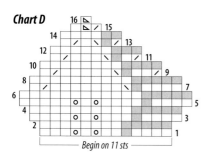

Begin on 11 sts

Chart C

Begin on 20 sts

Chart B

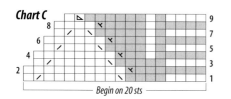

Begin on 23 sts

Chart A

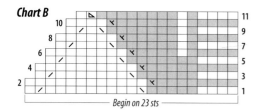

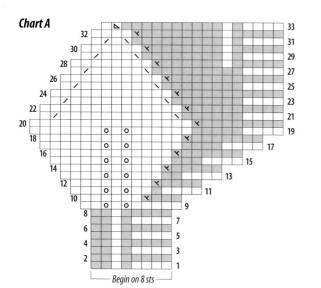

Begin on 8 sts

Stitch key
- ☐ K on RS, p on WS
- ▨ P on RS, k on WS
- ⊙ Yarn over
- ⊠ K in front and back of st
- ◣ Ssk
- ◿ K2tog on RS
- ◿ K2tog on WS
- ◤ SK2P on RS, SP2P on WS

more, then work rows 1–2 once more. Bind off. With crochet hook, work slip st across top of bound-off row, working ch-6 button loops to correspond to 10 neckline buttons.

Place Sequin (WS) Slip sequin onto crochet hook, pick up next st from left-hand needle onto crochet hook and slide sequin over st, making sure sequin stays at RS of work (see illustration). Place st back on left-hand needle and knit.

COBWEB COLLAR (photo, page 93)
26 (27, 28, 29, 31)" long x 4" wide
Cast on 199 (208, 214, 226, 247) sts. **Row 1** (RS) K1 through back loop (tbl), *p2, k1tbl; repeat from*. **Row 2** P1, *k1tbl, k1, p1; repeat from*. **Rows 3–18** Repeat rows 1 and 2 eight times more. **Row 19** K1tbl, *drop next st from LH needle, p1, k1tbl; repeat from*—133 (139, 143, 151, 165) sts. **Row 20** P1, *k1tbl, p1; repeat from*. **Row 21** K1tbl, *p1, k1tbl; repeat from*. **Rows 22 and 23** Repeat rows 20 and 21. Bind off in pattern. With crochet hook, work slip st across top of bound-off row, working ch-6 button loops to correspond to 10 neckline buttons. Unravel sts dropped in row 19 to cast-on row. Sew a bead at end of each knit rib.

LEAF COLLAR (photo, page 94)
29" long x 2½" wide
(Work collar using 1 strand yarn and 1 strand blending filament held together.)
Left side
kf&b Knit in front and back of a stitch.
SK2P Slip 1 knitwise, knit next 2 stitches together (k2tog), pass slipped stitch over the k2tog.
SP2P Slip 1 knitwise, purl next 2 stitches together (p2tog), pass slipped stitch over the p2tog.

Cast on 8 sts. **Row 1** (RS) K4, p1, k1, p2. **Row 2** K2, p1, k5. [Repeat rows 1 and 2] 0 (0, 1, 1, 1) time more. **Sizes S, M only** Work rows 1–33 of Chart A—18 sts. **Bind-off row** (WS) P2tog, k1, pass first st over 2nd st (pfso), *k1, pfso; repeat from* until 7 sts remain on left-hand needle, k1, p1, k5—8 sts. *Work rows 9–18 of Chart A—23 sts. Work rows 1–11 of Chart B—16 sts. Work Bind-off row—8 sts. Repeat from* once more. Work rows 9–16 of Chart A—20 sts. Work rows 1–9 of Chart C—14 sts. Work Bind-off row—8 sts. Work rows 9 and 10 of Chart A—11 sts. Work rows 1–16 of Chart D. Fasten off last st.

Sizes L, XL only Work rows 1–33 of Chart A—18 sts. **Bind-off row** (WS) P2tog, k1, pass first st over 2nd st (pfso), *k1, pfso; repeat from* until 7 sts remain on left-hand needle, k1, p1, k5—8 sts. Work rows 9–33 of Chart A—18 sts. Work Bind-off row—8 sts. Work rows 9–18 of Chart A—23 sts. Work rows 1–11 of Chart B—16 sts. Work Bind-off row—8 sts. Work rows 9–16 of Chart A—20 sts. Work rows 1–9 of Chart C—14 sts. Work Bind-off row—8 sts. Work rows 9 and 10 of Chart A—11 sts. Work rows 1–16 of Chart D. Fasten off last st.

Size XXL only Work rows 1–33 of Chart A—18 sts. **Bind-off row** (WS) P2tog, k1, pass first st over 2nd st (pfso), *k1, pfso; repeat from* until 7 sts remain on left-hand needle, k1, p1, k5—8 sts. Work rows 9–33 of Chart A—18 sts. Work Bind-off row—8 sts. Work rows 9–18 of Chart A—23 sts. Work rows 1–11 of Chart B—16 sts. Work Bind-off row—8 sts. Work rows 9–18 of Chart A—23 sts. Work rows 1–11 of Chart B—16 sts. Work Bind-off row—8 sts. Work rows 9 and 10 of Chart A—11 sts. Work rows 1–16 of Chart D. Fasten off last st.

CHART A (Begin on 8 sts)
Row 1, 3, 5, 7 (RS) K4, p1, k1, p2.
Row 2, 4, 6, 8 K2, p1, k5.
Row 9 K5, yo, k1, yo, k2.
Row 10 P6, k in front and back of st (kf&b), k to end.
Row 11 K4, p1, k2, yo, k1, yo, k3.
Row 12 P8, kf&b, k to end.
Row 13 K4, p2, k3, yo, k1, yo, k4.
Row 14 P10, kf&b, k to end.
Row 15 K4, p3, k4, yo, k1, yo, k5.
Row 16 P12, kf&b, k to end.
Row 17 K4, p4, k5, yo, k1, yo, k6.
Row 18 P14, kf&b, k to end.
Row 19 K4, p5, k6, yo, k1, yo, k7.
Row 20 P16, kf&b, k to end.
Row 21 K4, p6, ssk, k11, k2 tog, k1.
Row 22 P14, kf&b, k9.
Row 23 K4, p7, ssk, k9, k2tog, k1.
Row 24 P12, kf&b, k10.
Row 25 K4, p8, ssk, k7, k2tog, k1.
Row 26 P10, kf&b, k11.
Row 27 K4, p9, ssk, k5, k2tog, k1.
Row 28 P8, kf&b, k6, p1, k5.
Row 29 K4, p1, k1, p8, ssk, k3, k2tog, k1.
Row 30 P6, kf&b, k7, p1, k5.
Row 31 K4, p1, k1, p9, ssk, k1, k2tog, k1.
Row 32 P4, kf&b, k8, p1, k5.
Row 33 K4, p1, k1, p10, sk2p, k1.

CHART B (Begin on 23 sts)
Row 1 K4, p5, ssk, k9 k2tog, k1.
Row 2 P12, kf&b, k8.
Row 3 K4, p6, ssk, k7, k2tog, k1.
Row 4 P10, kf&b, k9.
Row 5 K4, p7, ssk, k5, k2tog, k1.
Row 6 P8, kf&b, k4, p1, k5.
Row 7 K4, p1, k1, p6, ssk, k3, k2tog, k1.
Row 8 P6, kf&b, k5, p1, k5.
Row 9 K4, p1, k1, p7, ssk, k1 k2tog, k1.
Row 10 P4, kf&b, k6, p1, k5.
Row 11 K4, p1, k1, p8, sk2p, k1.

CHART C (Begin on 20 sts)
Row 1 K4, p4, ssk, k7, k2tog, k1.
Row 2 P10, kf&b, k7.
Row 3 K4, p5, ssk, k5, k2tog, k1.
Row 4 P8, kf&b, k2, p1, k5.
Row 5 K4, p1, k1, p4, ssk, k3, k2tog, k1.
Row 6 P6, kf&b, k3, p1, k5.
Row 7 K4, p1, k1, p5, ssk, k1, k2tog, k1.
Row 8 P4, kf&b, k4, p1, k5.
Row 9 K4, p1, k1, p6, SK2P, k1.

CHART D (Begin on 11 sts)
Row 1 K4, p1, k2, yo, k1, yo, k3.
Row 2 P8, k5.
Row 3 K4, p1, k3, yo, k1, yo, k4.
Row 4 P10, k5.
Row 5 K4, p1, k4, yo, k1, yo, k5.
Row 6 P12, k5.
Row 7 K4, p1, ssk, k7, k2tog, k1.
Row 8 P10, k5.
Row 9 K2tog, k2, p1, ssk, k5, k2tog, k1.
Row 10 P8, k4.
Row 11 K2tog, k1, p1, ssk, k3, k2tog, k1.
Row 12 P6, k3.
Row 13 K2tog, p1, ssk, k1, k2tog, k1.
Row 14 P4, k2.
Row 15 K2tog, SK2P, k1.
Row 16 SP2P.

Right Side

Cast on 8 sts. *Row 1* (RS) P2, k1, p1, k4. *Row 2* K5, p1, k2. [Repeat rows 1 and 2] 0 (0, 1, 1, 1) time more.

Sizes S, M only Work rows 1–34 of Chart E—17 sts.
Bind-off row (RS) Bind off sts purlwise until 7 sts remain on left-hand needle, [k1, yo] twice, k5—10 sts. *Work rows 10–18 of Chart E—23 sts. Work rows 1–12 of Chart F—15 sts. Work Bind-off row—10 sts. Repeat from* once more. Work rows 10–16 of Chart E—20 sts. Work rows 1–10 of Chart G—13 sts. Work Bind-off row—10 sts. *Next row* (WS) K3, k into front and back of next st, p6—11 sts. Work rows 1–16 of Chart H. Fasten off last st.

Sizes L, XL only Work rows 1–34 of Chart E—17 sts.
Bind-off row (WS) Bind off sts purlwise until 7 sts remain on left-hand needle, [k1, yo] twice, k5—10 sts. Work rows 9–34 of Chart E—17 sts. Work Bind-off row—10 sts. Work rows 10–18 of Chart E—23 sts. Work rows 1–12 of Chart F—15 sts. Work Bind-off row—10 sts. Work rows 10–16 of Chart E—20 sts. Work rows 1–10 of Chart G—13 sts. Work Bind-off row—10 sts. *Next row* (WS) K3, k into front and back of next st, p6—11 sts. Work rows 1–16 of Chart H. Fasten off last st.

Size XXL only Work rows 1–34 of Chart E—17 sts.
Bind-off row (WS) Bind off sts purlwise until 7 sts rem on left-hand needle, [k1, yo] twice, k5—10 sts. Work rows 9–34 of Chart E—17 sts. Work Bind-off row—10 sts. *Work rows 10–18 of Chart E—23 sts. Work rows 1–12 of Chart F—15 sts. Work Bind-off row—10 sts. Repeat from* once more. *Next row* (WS) K3, k into front and back of next st, p6—11 sts. Work rows 1–16 of Chart H. Fasten off last st.

All sizes Use the yo in each leaf nearest the collar border as a buttonhole to fasten collar to body.

CHART E (Begin on 8 sts)

Row 1, 3, 5, 7 P2, k1, p1, k4.
Row 2, 4, 6, 8 K5, p1, k2.
Row 9 K2, yo, k1, yo, k5.
Row 10 K3, kf&b, p6.
Row 11 K3, yo, k1, yo, k2, p1, k4.
Row 12 K4, kf&b, p8.
Row 13 K4, yo, k1, yo, k3, p2, k4.
Row 14 K4, kf&b, k1, p10.
Row 15 K5, yo, k1, yo, k4, p3, k4.
Row 16 K4, kf&b, k2, p12.
Row 17 K6, yo, k1, yo, k5, p4, k4.
Row 18 k4, kf&b, k3, p14.
Row 19 K7, yo, k1, yo, k6, p5, k4.
Row 20 K4, kf&b, k4, p16.
Row 21 K1, ssk, k11, k2tog, p6, k4.
Row 22 K4, kf&b, k5, p14.
Row 23 K1, ssk, k9, k2tog, p7, k4.
Row 24 K4, kf&b, k6, p12.
Row 25 K1, ssk, k7, k2tog, p8, k4.
Row 26 K4, kf&b, k7, p10.
Row 27 K1, ssk, k5, k2tog, p9, k4.
Row 28 K5, p1, kf&b, k6, p8.
Row 29 K1, ssk, k3, k2tog, p8, k1, p1, k4.
Row 30 K5, p1, kf&b, k7, p6.
Row 31 K1, ssk, k1, k2tog, p9, k1, p1, k4.
Row 32 K5, p1, kf&b, k8, p4.
Row 33 K1, SK2P, p10, k1, p1, k4.
Row 34 K5, p1, k10, k2tog.

CHART F (Begin on 23 sts)

Row 1 K1, ssk, k9, k2tog, p5, k4.
Row 2 K4, fk&b, k4, p12.
Row 3 K1, ssk, k7, k2tog, p6, k4.
Row 4 K4, kf&b, k5, p10.
Row 5 K1, ssk, k5, k2tog, p7, k4.
Row 6 K5, p1, kf&b, k4, p8.
Row 7 K1, ssk, k3, k2tog, p6, k1, p1, k4.
Row 8 K5, p1, kf&b, k5, p6.
Row 9 K1, ssk, k1, k2tog, p7, k1, p1, k4.
Row 10 K5, p1, kf&b, k6, p4.
Row 11 K1, SK2P, p8, k1, p1, k4.
Row 12 K5, p1, k8, k2tog.

CHART G (Begin on 20 sts)

Row 1 K1, ssk, k7, k2tog, p4, k4.
Row 2 K4, kf&b, k3, p10.
Row 3 K1, ssk, k5, k2tog, p5, k4.
Row 4 K5, p1, kf&b, k2, p8.
Row 5 K1, ssk, k3, k2tog, p4, k1, p1, k4.
Row 6 K5, p1, kf&b, k3, p6.
Row 7 K1, ssk, k1, k2tog, p5, k1, p1, k4.
Row 8 K5, p1, kf&b, k4, p4.
Row 9 K1, SK2P, p6, k1, p1, k4.
Row 10 K5, p1, k6, k2tog.

CHART H (Begin on 11 sts)

Row 1 K3, yo, k1, yo, k2, p1, k4.
Row 2 K5, p8.
Row 3 K4, yo, k1, yo, k3, p1, k4.
Row 4 K5, p10.
Row 5 K5, yo, k1, yo, k4, p1, k4.
Row 6 K5, p12.
Row 7 K1, ssk, k7, k2tog, p1, k4.
Row 8 K5, p10.
Row 9 K1, ssk, k5, k2tog, p1, k2, k2tog.
Row 10 K4, p8.
Row 11 K1, ssk, k3, k2tog, p1, k1, k2tog.
Row 12 K3, p6.
Row 13 K1, ssk, k1, k2tog, p1, k2tog.
Row 14 K2, p4.
Row 15 K1, SK2P, k2tog.
Row 16 SP2P.

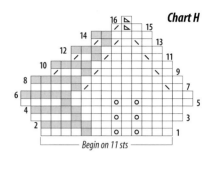

Chart H

Begin on 11 sts

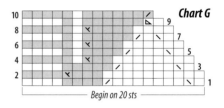

Chart G

Begin on 20 sts

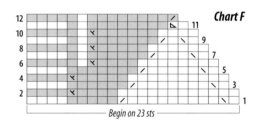

Chart F

Begin on 23 sts

Stitch key

☐ *K on RS, p on WS*
▨ *P on RS, k on WS*
○ *Yarn over*
⧖ *K in front and back of st*
╲ *Ssk*
╱ *K2tog on RS*
╱ *K2tog on WS*
◣ *SK2P on RS, SP2P on WS*

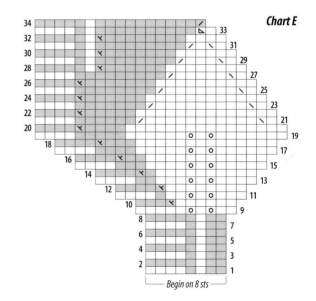

Chart E

Begin on 8 sts

Techniques

A few basic techniques are all that's needed to knit and finish most jackets. Occasionally, a recommended method may not be familiar, or it may be known by another name. The next few pages should answer any questions that arise.

LOOP CAST-ON

Uses To cast on a few sts for a buttonhole. Loops can slant either to the right or to the left. For right-slanting cast-on, work the next row through the back loop.

Left-slanting

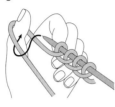

Right-slanting

LONG-TAIL CAST-ON

Make a slipknot for the initial stitch, at a distance from the end of the yarn (about 1½" for each stitch to be cast on).

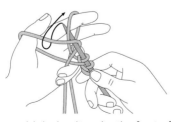

1 Arrange both ends of yarn in left hand as shown. Bring needle under front strand of thumb loop, up over front strand of index loop, catching it . . .

2. . . and bringing it under the front of the thumb loop. Slip thumb out of loop, and use it to adjust tension on the new stitch. One stitch cast on.

CABLE CAST-ON

Uses A cast-on that is useful when adding stitches within the work.

1 Place a slipknot on left needle.

2 Working into this knot's loop, knit a stitch and place it on left needle.

3 Insert right needle between the last 2 stitches. From this position, knit a stitch and place it on left needle. Repeat step 3 for each additional stitch.

LIFTED INCREASE

Uses A single increase.

1 With right needle from back of work, pick up strand between last st knitted and next st. Place on left needle and knit, twisting the strand by working into the loop at the back of the needle.

2 This is the completed increase.

ONE-ROW BUTTONHOLE

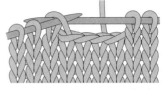

1 At marker, bring the yarn to the front and slip the next stitch purlwise. Put the yarn to the back and leave it there. *Slip the next stitch purlwise, then pass the previously slipped stitch over it; repeat from* for each buttonhole stitch. Slip the last bound-off stitch to the left needle and turn work.

2 Bring the yarn to the back and cast on using the cable cast-on as follows: *Insert the right needle between the first and second stitches on the left needle, wrap the yarn as if to knit, pull the loop through and place it on the left needle; repeat from* until you have cast on one stitch more than was bound off. Turn work.

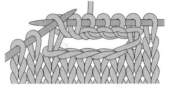

3 Bring the yarn to the back, slip the first stitch from the left needle and pass the extra cast-on stitch over it and tighten firmly.

BUTTONHOLE PLACEMENT

Often you are given specific instructions for placing the top and bottom buttons. To place the remaining buttons evenly between these two, measure the distance and divide by the number of remaining buttons plus 1. If five buttons remain, divide the distance (say 15") by 5 + 1; 15 divided by 6 equals 2.5: position a button centered every 2.5".

Techniques

SSK

Uses A left-slanting single decrease.

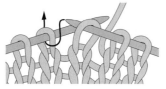

1 Slip 2 sts separately to right needle as if to knit.

2 Knit these 2 sts together by slipping left needle into them from left to right; 2 sts become one.

SK2P, SL1-K2TOG-PSSO

Uses A left-slanting double decrease.
1 Slip one stitch knitwise.
2 Knit next two stitches together.
3 Pass the slipped stitch over the k2tog.

4 Completed: 3 sts become 1; the right st is on top.

SP2P, SL1-P2TOG-PSSO

Uses A left-slanting double decrease.
1 Slip one stitch knitwise.
2 Purl next two stitches together.
3 Pass the slipped stitch over the p2tog.

SINGLE CROCHET (SC)

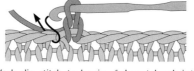

Work slip stitch to begin. **1** Insert hook into next stitch.

2 Yarn over and through stitch; 2 loops on hook.

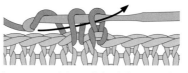

3 Yarn over and through both loops on hook; single crochet completed. Repeat Steps 1-3.

DOUBLE YARN OVER (YO)

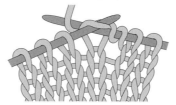

Wrap yarn twice around needle between stitches.

K1B

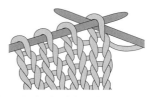

Knit through the back loop (k1b)

To knit into the back of a stitch, insert the needle into the stitch from right to left.

CRAB STITCH

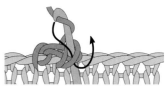

1 Work from left to right. **1a** Work a slip stitch to begin. **1b** Enter hook into next stitch to right.

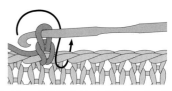

2 Bring yarn through stitch only. As soon as hook clears the stitch, flip your wrist (and the hook). There are now two loops on the hook, and the just-made loop is to the front of the hook (left of the old loop).

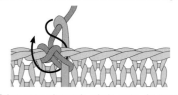

3 Yarn over and through both loops on hook; one backward single crochet completed.

4 Continue working to right, repeating from Step 1b.

GRAFTING

Uses An invisible method of joining knitting horizontally, row to row. Useful at shoulders, underarms, and tips of mittens, socks, and hats.

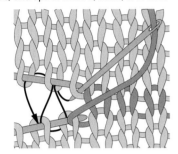

Stockinette graft

1 Arrange stitches on two needles.

2 Thread a blunt needle with matching yarn (approximately 1" per stitch).

3 Working from right to left, with right sides facing you, begin with Steps 3a and 3b:

3a Front needle: yarn through 1st stitch as if to purl, leave stitch on needle.

3b Back needle: yarn through 1st stitch as if to knit, leave on.

4 Work 4a and 4b across:

4a Front needle: through 1st stitch as if to knit, slip off needle; through next st as if to purl, leave on needle.

4b Back needle: through 1st stitch as if to purl, slip off needle; through next st as if to knit, leave on needle.

5 Adjust tension to match rest of knitting.

3-NEEDLE BIND-OFF

Uses Instead of binding off shoulder stitches and sewing them together.

Place right sides together, back stitches on one needle and front stitches on another. *K2tog (1 from front needle and 1 from back needle). Rep from* once. Pass first stitch over 2nd stitch. Continue to k2tog (1 front stitch and 1 back stitch) and bind off across.

CHAIN STITCH (CH)

Make slip knot.

1 Yarn over hook.

2 Draw yarn through loop on hook. Repeat Steps 1 and 2 for each additional chain stitch.

SLIP STITCH

1 Insert the crochet hook into the fabric, catch the yarn, and pull up a loop.

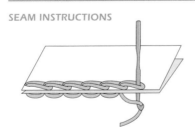

2 Go into the next stitch of the fabric and draw a new loop through the fabric and the loop on the hook, leaving one loop on the hook. Make each loop a little loose so the edge won't be tight. Repeat this step to the end.

SEAM INSTRUCTIONS

In this book, unless the pattern advises another method, work all seams by placing right sides of pieces together and slip stitch crocheting through both layers, working between the edge stitch and the next stitch. Use the yarn the garment was knitted with unless it is difficult to work with (too heavy, too textured, or too fragile). In that case, use a yarn (finer, smoother, or stronger) in a similar color and fiber.

ABBREVIATIONS

b	back
CC	contrasting color
ch	chain
cm	centimeter(s)
dpn(s)	double-pointed needle(s)
k	knit
L	large
M1	make one increase
m	meter(s)
M	medium
MC	main color
mm	millimeter(s)
p	purl
pm	place marker
psso	pass slipped stitch over
rep	repeat
rnd(s)	round(s)
RS	right side
sc	single crochet
sl	slip(ping)
S	small
st(s)	stitch(es)
St st	stockinette stitch
tog	together
WS	wrong side
wyib	with yarn in back
wyif	with yarn in front
X(L)(S)	extra(large)(small)
XXL	extra extra large
yd	yard
yo	yarn over
"	inches

Fabric

Knit fabric is a fusion of stitch, yarn, and gauge. This section highlights the first element: combinations of knit, purl, and slip that create interest whether worked in one color or more. These versatile stitches are easy to knit and give a jacket the body it needs.

Stitches

What gives a knitted fabric the body most jacket styles need? Certainly gauge and yarn choice contribute, but the architecture of the fabric—its structure of knits, purls, and other simple manipulations of stitches—is the determining factor.

SIMPLE STITCHES

We begin this book with four jackets that use stockinette stitch: the first two are in smooth yarns with the knit side as the right side, the next two are worked in textured yarns with the purl side as the right side. The latter, reverse stockinette, is especially effective with boucle and other textured yarns.

The remainder of the jackets use pattern stitches—some are worked in a single color and the interest is the texture; in others, the focus is on the interplay of two or more colors. The next few pages highlight a few of each. Try knitting a swatch of any that are unfamiliar. Pick a favorite. Experiment.

TEXTURE

The Basket Weave and Twill patterns are just stockinette stitch with some of the stitches slipped while the yarn is carried on the right side. These horizontal carries form patterns that resemble woven fabrics.

The Rice pattern is a quasi-rib: wrong-side rows are knit, right-side rows are knit 1 (in the back loop), purl 1 rib. It turns a plain yarn into a beautifully nubby fabric.

The Tweed pattern is a little tricky, but once learned, it works very smoothly. It takes on new life when worked in a tweed yarn.

Slipping, twisting, and crossing compress the stitches and rows of these textured patterns, producing the firm yet flexible fabric that gives body to a knitted jacket.

COLOR

Slip stitches truly shine when a second or third color is introduced. Three of the stitches we feature are related: they use garter and slip stitches to produce small block patterns. The yarn color changes every other row, and the same stitch is slipped (with the yarn on the wrong side, this time) for two rows. The simple shifting of stitches and a change in color, type, and even weight of one of the yarns can change their appearance dramatically. Try a textured yarn with a smooth one; mix fibers (Atherton, page 42, combines linen with mohair) or weights of yarn; try strong or muted color contrast. In the fourth feature, linen stitch, every other stitch is slipped every row; the stitches that aren't slipped are worked in stockinette. The yarn color changes every row, so three colors work best. This stitch rivals any woven fabric in firmness, and, for a jacket, is best knit in a fine weight yarn (see chart on page 113).

Don't let the intricate, multicolored appearance of these stitches intimidate you. They are very easy to knit. Only one color is used in any row.

Firmer fabric means more yarn, more knitting. Both garter and slipped stitches compress the knitting vertically, and slipped stitches stabilize the width of the fabric. This does translate into more rows to work, but since a good portion of the stitches are just slipped from one needle to the other, the knitting goes more quickly and easily than the row gauge would imply.

All these stitches create wonderfully wearable, durable fabrics that appeal to the eye and hand using readily available, classic yarns of light to medium weight. In other words, they can turn meat-and-potato basics into gourmet fabrics. Enjoy!

Edgings

- *The edging is an important part of the design process and of the finished garment. It frames the jacket.*

- *A stockinette stitch rolled edge in the main or a contrasting color can be worked on the cast-on stitches for each section and knitted onto front and neck edges at the end.*

- *Simply working one garter ridge before beginning the pattern stitch may be all that's needed. This ridge can be added to other edges by picking up stitches, knitting one row, and binding off.*

- *If the fabric already lays flat, mimic its cast-on edge along the front and neck opening by picking up stitches and binding them off on the same row.*

- *Several rows of single crochet make a nice finish. Or consider one row of Crab stitch (single crochet worked backwards, from left to right).*

- *If you do not like the edging called for in a pattern, substitute one of these or invent one of your own. Test edge treatments on your gauge swatch.*

Basket weave pattern

Trilling 06, page 22

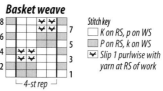

Basket weave

Stitch key
☐ K on RS, p on WS
☒ P on RS, k on WS
☒ Slip 1 purlwise with yarn at RS of work

4-st rep

(multiple of 4 sts; includes edge sts)
Row 1 (RS) K1, *k2, p2; repeat from*, end k1.
Row 2 K1, *k2, p2; repeat from*, end k1.
Row 3 K1, *k2, slip 2 purlwise with yarn in front (sl2 wyif); repeat from*, end k1.
Row 4 K1, *slip 2 purlwise with yarn in back (sl2 wyib)p2; repeat from*, end k1.
Row 5 Repeat row 2.
Row 6 Repeat row 1.
Row 7 K1, *sl2 wyif, k2; repeat from*, end k1.
Row 8 K1, *p2, sl2 wyib; repeat from*, end k1.

Twill pattern

Clarendon 16, page 64

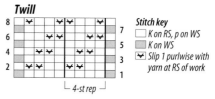

Twill

Stitch key
☐ K on RS, p on WS
☒ K on WS
☒ Slip 1 purlwise with yarn at RS of work

4-st rep

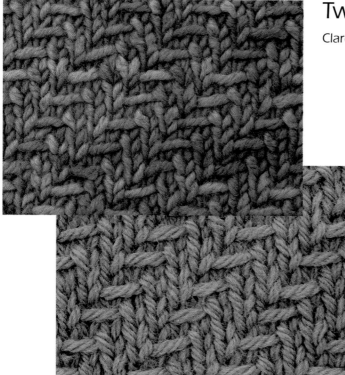

(multiple of 4 sts plus 2; includes edge sts)
Row 1 and all WS rows K1, p across; end k1.
Row 2 (RS) K1, *k2, slip 2 with yarn in front (sl2 wyif); repeat from*, end k1.
Row 4 K2, *sl2 wyif, k2; repeat from*.
Row 6 K1, *sl2 wyif, k2; repeat from*, end k3.
Row 8 K1, sl1 wyif, *k2, sl2 wyif; repeat from*, end k2, sl1 wyif, k1.

Rice pattern

Copley 07, page 26

A very reversible fabric: wrong side shown here and on front cover; right side on pages 26-29

Rice

Stitch key
☐ K on RS, p on WS
▨ P on RS, k on WS
B K in back of st

(multiple of 2 sts plus 1; includes edge sts)
Row 1 (WS) K.
Row 2 K1, *p1, k1 in back of st; repeat from*, end p1, k1.

TEXTURE

Tweed pattern

Gloucester 17, page 68

(multiple of 2; includes edge sts)
Row 1 (RS) K2, *sl1, k1, yo, pass sl st over both k1 and yo; repeat from*, end k2.
Row 2 K1, *p1 in 2nd st without removing st from left-hand needle, then p in first st. Slip both sts from left-hand needle; repeat from*, end k1.
Row 3 K.
Row 4 K1, p to last st, k1.

103

Garter slip pattern

Claridge 09, page 34

Garter Slip

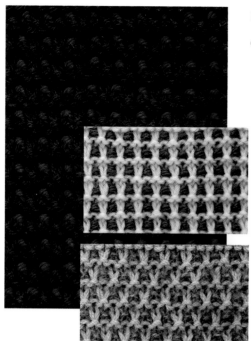

(multiple of 2 sts plus 1; includes edge sts)
Row 1, 2 With MC, k.
Row 3 (RS) With CC, k2, *slip 1 st purlwise with yarn in back (sl 1 wyib), k1; repeat from*, end k2.
Row 4 With CC, k2, *slip 1 st purlwise with yarn in front (sl 1 wyif), k1; repeat from*, end k2.
Row 5, 6 With MC, k.
Row 7 With CC, k1, *sl 1 wyib, k1; repeat from*, end k2.
Row 8 With CC, k1, *sl 1 wyif, k1; repeat from*, end k2.

Color key
☐ MC
▨ CC

Stitch key
☐ K on RS
▭ K on WS
☑ Slip 1 purlwise with yarn at WS of work

3-color Tweed pattern

Devonshire 10, page 38

(multiple of 3 sts plus 1; includes edge sts)
Row 1 (RS) With A, k3, *slip 1 purlwise with yarn in back (sl 1 wyib), k2; repeat from*, end k1.
Row 2 With A, k3, *sl 1 purlwise with yarn in front (sl 1 wyif), k2; repeat from*, end k1.
Row 3 With B, *k2, sl 1 wyib; repeat from*, end k1.
Row 4 With B, k1, *sl 1 wyif, k2; repeat from*.
Row 5 With MC, k1, *sl 1 wyib, k2; repeat from*.
Row 6 With MC, k2, *sl 1 wyif, k2; repeat from*, end sl 1 wyif, k1.

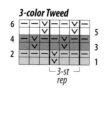

3-color Tweed

Color key
☐ MC
▨ B
▨ A

Stitch key
☐ K on RS, p on WS
▭ P on RS, k on WS
☑ Slip 1 purlwise with yarn at WS of work

Fabric stitch

Atherton 11, page 42

(multiple of 2 plus 1; includes edge sts)
Row 1 (RS) With MC, k.
Row 2 With MC, k.
Row 3 With CC, k2, *slip 1 purlwise with
yarn in back (sl 1 wyib), k1; repeat from*, end k2.
Row 4 With CC, k2, *slip 1 purlwise with
yarn in front (sl 1 wyif), k1; repeat from*, end k2.

Fabric

Color key
☐ MC
▨ CC

Stitch key
☐ K on RS
— K on WS
☑ Slip 1 purlwise with
yarn at WS of work

COLOR

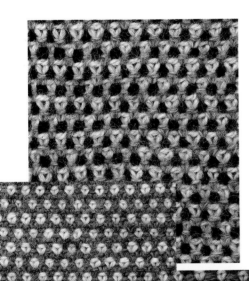

Linen pattern

Winchester 12, page 46

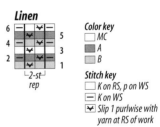

Linen

Color key
☐ MC
▨ A
▨ B

Stitch key
☐ K on RS, p on WS
— K on WS
☑ Slip 1 purlwise with
yarn at RS of work

(Multiple of 2; includes edge sts)
Row 1 (RS) With B, k1, *k1, slip 1 st purlwise with yarn
in front (sl 1 wyif); repeat from*, k1.
Row 2 With A, k1, *p1, sl 1 purlwise with yarn in back (sl
1 wyib); repeat from*, k1.
Row 3 With MC, repeat row 1.
Row 4 With B, repeat row 2.
Row 5 With A, repeat row 1.
Row 6 With MC, repeat row 2.

105

Fit & fiber

When knitting a jacket (or any garment), knowledge of one's body measurements is of prime importance. Although sizes in magazines and books are standardized—based on average measurements, few of us find standard sizes an exact fit. That is why each knitter should be aware of her own measurements. This information makes it easier to choose or design an appropriately sized pattern and to customize its fit, if necessary.

Fit & size

Women's sizes						
	XS	**Small**	**Medium**	**Large**	**XL**	**XXL**
Actual bust	28–30"	32–34"	36–38"	40–42"	44–46"	48–50"
Standard-fitting	32"	36"	40"	44"	48"	52"
Loose-fitting	34"	38"	42"	46"	50"	54"
Waist length	16½"	17"	17¼"	17½"	17¾"	18"
Hip length	22½"	23"	23¼"	23½"	23¾"	24"

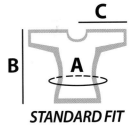

STANDARD FIT

FINISHED measurements
Women's S (M, L)
A 41½ (45, 48½)"
B 18 (19, 22)"
C 28¼ (30, 30¼)"

Two types of fit are used for the jackets: standard fit, with up to 4 inches of ease, and loose, with 6 or more inches. Ease is important for fit as you will be wearing the jackets over blouses and tops.

We offer jackets for women sized from XS to XXL (28–50" bust), and although none of the patterns cover the complete range, you will find jackets that work for you, in your size.

Due to stitch pattern repeats and fabric considerations, ease differs between jacket styles. The fit icon in each pattern (and shown here) shows 3 measurements: *A* bust, *B* jacket length, *C* sleeve length.

The schematics in each pattern (and shown below) provide measurements for the garment pieces. You can make sure each dimension works for you and check each piece as it is knit.

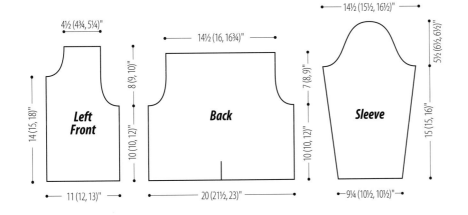

Taking measurements

Take your measurements over light clothing and have someone assist you.

Across back (shoulder to shoulder)
Let's start at the top. Your shoulders are the "hanger" for your jacket, so it is important that the shoulder area fits properly. Feel your shoulder: at the top of your arm you will find a prominent bone where the arm joins the shoulder. Measure the distance across the back between these two bones to obtain the shoulder width.

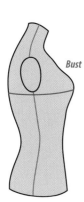

✷ Bust
The bust measurement must be taken at its fullest part. Do not take this measurement too tightly; a finger or two under the tape will give a bit of ease. The tape measure should run parallel to the floor (not raised in the back).

Divide the total measurement in half to determine front and back widths. If you have a large bust, separate the measurement in two unequal parts: across front side seam to side seam, and across back side seam to side seam. If the front width is significantly larger than the back, see *Making it fit* on page 110 for suggestions on customizing pattern fit.

Waist
The waist measurement is not required if the jacket's side seams are straight from the hem to the armhole. However, it is important in a fitted garment. Place the tape around the waistline with a couple of fingers beneath the tape in order to obtain a relaxed measurement. While the tape is around the waist, use another tape to measure the center back length from the prominent bone at the base of the neck to the waist.

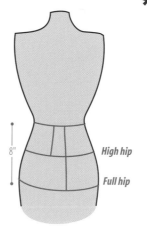

✷ Hips
Take four measurements for the hips. The first, the full hip measurement, should be taken at the widest point of the hips, (usually about eight inches below the waist). Again relax the tape a bit. The second measurement, referred to as the high hip, should be taken approximately half way between the waistline and the full hip. Third and fourth, find the length at the center back between the waist and both hip measurements. These measurements are important for a fitted jacket that is to be hip-bone length or longer.

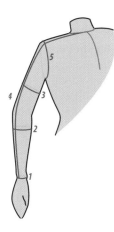

* Arm

Let's start at the bottom and take five measurements. Measure the circumference at the wrist bone for a cuff measurement (1). Measure around the forearm at its fullest point between the elbow and the wrist (2). Measure around the upper arm at its fullest part (3). The best way to measure arm length is to have your arm resting to your side and slightly bent. Measure the length from the wrist bone around the slightly bent elbow to the shoulder point and across to the center back (4). (This is the **C** measurement shown on each pattern's fit icon—see the example on page 107—and is how sleeve length is measured for menswear, too.) We also need the armscye or armhole circumference. Measure the distance from the shoulder down, around, under the arm, and back up to the shoulder (5). (This distance may be easier to measure using a well-fitting garment.)

Your measurements

Across back ....
Shoulder to shoulder

Width of each shoulder, and neck ....
Divide width of shoulder by 3; an approximation

* **Bust** ....

Waist ....

Back length ....
Neck bone to waist

High hip ....

* **High hip to waist** ....

Full hip ....

Full hip to waist ....

Wrist ....

Forearm ....
at fullest part

Upper arm ....
at fullest part

* **Arm** ....
Length from wrist to center back; arm should be slightly bent

Armsyce ....
(armhole circumference)

Use pencil to note your measurements in the chart so that if you change size, the entries can be easily changed.

*These measurements relate to the Fit measurements in each pattern.

Making it fit

Pattern measurements are standardized (see the chart on page 107), but individuals often do not conform exactly to that standard. Pick the size with bust, waist, and hip measurements closest to yours. If your measurements don't all match a size, usually it is best to select the size closest to your bust measurement. You may not need to make any adjustments to the pattern, but minor adjustments to a standard size are often all that is needed to give a knitted jacket a custom fit.

Shoulder

The most critical area of fit in a jacket pattern is the shaping from bust to shoulders. A larger bust doesn't always mean a wider measurement across the back (shoulder to shoulder). Compare your shoulder width to that given on the schematic for the pattern. The goal is to have the sleeve seam rest on the shoulder-to-arm joint. If the pattern is too wide at the shoulder, you may need to remove more stitches at the armscye (armhole shaping). If the pattern is too narrow at the shoulder, you may need to remove fewer stitches. Your sleeve will need to reflect those changes.

These jackets are designed for a tailored look; squared shoulders and firm fabrics support this. If your shoulders are narrow and/or sloped and you find the need for shoulder pads, please add them to your jacket to maintain the look.

Bust

If you have a full bust—a D cup or larger—you may want to make your jacket front a bit wider than your jacket back. Check your front width and back width measurements. Add extra width to the fronts (maybe an inch, or one repeat of the pattern, to each front piece), and then remove the extra stitches at the armscye through additional decreases (continue decreases at the same rate until the additional stitches have been decreased away).

Hips

If your hips are larger than standard, cast on the additional stitches needed and decrease them out by the time you reach the armscye, creating a slightly A-line shape.

In most cases, if your hips are smaller than standard, it will not require an adjustment.

Waist

Most jackets are straight from hip to bust. Should you choose a jacket with a fitted waist, you need to consider your length to waist and waist measurements. Adjustments can be made for either. Adjust the placement of the first and last decrease and increase rounds if necessary to reflect your back length to waist and full hip to waist length. Adjust the number (and spacing) of decrease and increase rounds to accommodate a larger waist.

In most cases, a waist smaller than standard does not require an adjustment.

Yarn requirements

Finally, don't forget this very important consideration: while making these changes, remember your yarn requirements may change—more inches means more yarn.

Stitch gauge

Next to knowing your individual measurements, the most essential factor in making a knit fit is getting gauge.

The pattern calls for a weight of yarn, needle size, and the number of stitches. But not everyone knits the same size stitches with the same needles and yarn weight—some knit loosely, others knit tightly. This is why patterns specify gauge: the number of stitches and rows to 10cm/4".

By knitting a sample (swatch), washing it as you will your garment, measuring it, and counting how many stitches fit within 10cm/4", you determine your gauge. If your gauge does not match the gauge given in the pattern, then make additional swatches, using whatever needle size is necessary to attain the gauge specified in the pattern. Getting gauge is crucial to knitting a garment of a specified size.

If you get too few stitches per inch, you need to use smaller (thinner) needles to obtain the suggested gauge. If you get too many, use larger (thicker) needles. Continue swatching until you find the proper needles for the gauge.

Stitches count

As an experiment, cast on enough stitches to make a swatch approximately 6" wide and work for approximately 2" in height with the suggested needle size, then go up a needle size and knit another 2", then 2" with a needle smaller than the original. Carefully measure across 4" in the center of each section and place a pin at the end of the 4" area. Count the stitches between the pins. You will get different counts in each section, and you will see that the width of the swatch changes as this count changes.

What gauge can mean in a garment

• The pattern gauge is 24 stitches to 10cm/4". The gauge of your swatch is 24 stitches to 10cm/4" (6 stitches to the inch). The back of the garment is 126 stitches wide. The back measurement would be 21" (126 divided by 6 = 21"), resulting in a 42" circumference garment.
• But if your swatch gauge is 5.5 stitches to 1" and you divided 126 by 5.5, the back would measure 22.9" or 45.8" around.
• And if the swatch gauge is 6.5 stitches to 1", the back would be 19.4" wide or 38.8" around.

What might seem to be a small difference in gauge can result in a dramatic difference (plus or minus 3 or 4") in size.

Rows count

Your swatch is also used to measure row count. If you are having trouble exactly matching both stitch and row gauge, row gauge is often not as critical.

Pattern stitches have row repeats; most patterns used in this book are small, so a few extra rows will not affect the overall look of the garment. If the row repeat is large, consideration has been given as to where to interrupt it so as not ruin the effect of the repeat when adjusting the length of the garment.

Making the most of your swatch

A swatch also shows you how a stitch pattern works. If you don't enjoy working the stitch, find another! It is not worth your time to work on something you do not like. Perfect your finishing techniques, trims, and other details on the swatch before you invest time on the project.

32 ⬚ 24 GET GAUGE!

Yarn

Selecting yarn for a knitting project involves the consideration of many factors. The choice of color, fiber content, texture, and weight—properties that elicit an immediate sensual response—should be balanced with the practical concerns of cost, garment care, and suitability for the project. A knitter makes conscious decisions, but not without being influenced by emotion.

1 2 3 **4** 5 6

Medium weight

Color
Often, color is what first attracts us to a yarn. We respond to color from across a room, and we are drawn to those that flatter or excite us.

Texture
The sense of touch is constantly involved in knitting. We choose a yarn not only because we want a knitted fabric that feels nice to wear, but also because we will spend many hours knitting with it, and that experience should be pleasant.

Content
The fiber composition influences the yarn's look, feel, and behavior. The drape and memory of a finished fabric, as well as its surface reflectivity (matte or shine) depend on fiber type. Insulative qualities and ease of care also affect yarn selection.

Weight
Generally, the thickness of the yarn determines the thickness of the fabric and the amount of time required to create it. A fabric made of fine yarn on small needles will have more stitches and rows, finer detail, and a different drape than fabric knit with heavier yarn on larger needles—and it will take more time and patience.

Construction
Yarns can be spun into anything from a smooth "classic" to a fanciful delight of strands and fibers. The number of plies (strands), from one to many, as well as the firmness of the spinning can influence stitch definition. Brushing, overtwisting, looping, knotting, and knarling produce an endless array of color and texture effects.

Cost
Price doesn't always ensure quality. Buy quality yarn, and make sure it will suit your project and knitting desires. Resist purchasing yarns that are not enjoyable to knit, regardless of price.

Care
Different fibers require different care. Check the yarn label for the manufacturer's recommendations. Cottons can be machine washed and dried, while silks should be dry cleaned to maintain their color. Wools should never be machine washed, unless the yarn has been treated to withstand it. Synthetics are designed for easy care (but one still should be sensible). Always treat your swatch as you plan to treat the jacket.

When it comes to yarn selection, follow your eyes, your sense of touch, and your instincts. The experience you gain by knitting with a variety of yarns will help you make wise choices for your next knitting project.

Suppliers

Brown Sheep Co
100662 County Road 16
Mitchell, NE 69357
www.brownsheep.com

Louet Sales Inc
808 Commerce Park Dr
Ogdensburg, NY 13669
www.louet.com

Lion Brand
34 W 15th Street
New York, NY 10011
www.lionbrand.com

Muench Yarns Inc
285 Bel Marin Keys Blvd #J
Novato, CA 94949
www.muenchyarns.com

Bryson Distributing LLC
4065 W 11th Ave #39-40
Eugene, OR 97402
www.brysonknits.com

Wool in the Woods
58 Scarlet Way
Biglerville, PA 17307
www.woolinthewoods.com

Dale of Norway
N16 W23390
Stoneridge Dr. #A
Waukesha, WI 53186
www.daleofnorway.com

Tahki-Stacy Charles Inc
8000 Cooper Ave Bldg 1
Glendale, NY 11385
www.tahkistacycharles.com

Schaefer Yarn Co LTD
3514 Kelly's Corners
Interlaken, NY 14847
www.schaeferyarn.com

Plymouth Yarn Co
500 Lafayette Street
Bristol, PA 19007
www.plymouthyarn.com

**Trendsetter Yarns/
Lane Borgosesia**
16745 Saticoy St #101
Van Nuys, CA 91406

Yarn weights

Yarn Weight	**1** *Super Fine*	**2** *Fine*	**3** *Light*	**4** *Medium*	**5** *Bulky*	**6** *Super Bulky*
Also called	Sock Fingering Baby	Sport Baby	DK Light Worsted	Worsted Afghan	Chunky Craft Aran	Bulky Roving Rug
Stockinette Stitch Gauge Range 10cm/4 inches	27 to 32 sts	23 to 26 sts	21 to 24 sts	16 to 20 sts	12 to 15 sts	6 to 11 sts
Recommended Needle (metric)	2 mm to 3.25 mm	3.25 mm to 3.75 mm	3.75 mm to 4.5 mm	4.5 mm to 5.5 mm	5.5 mm to 8 mm	9 mm to 16 mm
Recommended Needle (US)	1 to 3	3 to 5	5 to 7	7 to 9	9 to 11	13 to 19

Locate the Yarn Weight and Stockinette Stitch Gauge Range over 10cm to 4" on the chart. Compare that range with the information on the yarn label to find an appropriate yarn.

Note: In this book, gauge is given over the stitch pattern used for the jacket and may vary considerably from that yarn's gauge over stockinette. This chart provides what you need when choosing a yarn—its gauge over stockinette.

Finishing

Finishing begins as you cast on the first stitch. Flawless knitting, proper blocking and seaming, and perfectly executed details make a sound and wearable garment. The following time-tested, practical finishing techniques will give your knit garment a better fit and a smooth, polished appearance.

SWATCH

Begin with a swatch. Wash and block it: soak the swatch in cool water, use the spin cycle of the washer to remove the excess water, then pat the piece into shape and allow it to dry. Treat the swatch just as you would the finished jacket. Wash and block each piece of knitting as it comes off the needles.

Garter edges

Knit the first and last stitch of every row in the swatch and the knitted garment pieces (see illustration) to form a neat edge that will make seaming effortless.

One-stitch garter edge

WS

KNITTING

Back

Knit the back of the jacket first. This piece is large enough to confirm the pattern calculations.

Fronts

Knit the left front next. It involves less work than the right front, which usually requires buttonholes. Use the left front to calculate the placement for buttons, and then work the right front with buttonholes to match (see illustration).

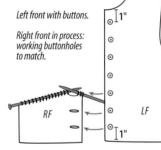

Left front with buttons.

Right front in process: working buttonholes to match.

RF   *LF*

Many designers use 5 to 7 buttons in a garment but you have the option of using any number you wish—just make sure to use enough to prevent a gap at the bust.

Sleeves

Knit the sleeves next, keeping the shaping consistent and neat by mirroring the increases and decreases inside the garter edges.

STRATEGY

Lay out the pieces and see what needs to be done. It is usually easier to apply pockets and such on pieces than on the whole garment, but that is a personal choice.

JOINS

Joins in knitting should be undetectable. Start new balls of yarn at side seams, and use careful, even stitching when tacking down facings, placing patch pockets, or adding a collar.

Pockets

If the pocket has a lining, pin the lining in place and sew it to the front, making sure it does not distort the fabric. If the pocket has a knitted or crocheted edge, apply it. Patch pockets are usually centered on the front, about one or two inches above the hem of the jacket (the pattern may specify exact placement) (see illustration).

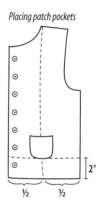

Placing patch pockets

2"

½   *½*

Trims and edges

Crochet trims or knitted edges frame your knitting and should be perfectly executed. Practice on a swatch until you like what you get—it's worth the time and effort.

Bands

Start with the left. If a front edge is knitted or crocheted, it must maintain gauge. Too many stitches will make the fronts droop and the edge ripple; too few will cause the fronts to hike up, pucker, and bow. If the band has a pattern repeat, you may need to adjust the multiple to make the repeat complete or balanced.

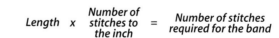

$$\text{Length} \times \frac{\text{Number of stitches to the inch}}{} = \frac{\text{Number of stitches required for the band}}{}$$

Buttons

If the buttons are to be sewn to the band, sew them now, to facilitate buttonhole placement on the right front band.

Placing buttons and buttonholes

- *Choose buttons that will accent your garment*
- *Work a buttonhole on your swatch to confirm the buttonhole size*
- *Knit the left front*
- *Place the top button ½ inch from the neck and mark the placement*
- *Place the bottom button about 2 inches from the hem and mark*
- *Space additional buttons evenly between top and bottom, and mark*
- *Sew on buttons*
- *Align buttonholes to buttons as you knit the right front*
- *Finish front edges with crochet, knit, or buttonband*

ASSEMBLY

Join the fronts to the back at the shoulders using a continuous bind-off. This provides a single, smooth seam that is firm yet flexible. The shoulder seams support the weight of the entire garment, and the three-needle bind-off helps prevent stretching, while allowing the garment to drape properly and without distortion. The seam can readily become part of a stitch pattern.

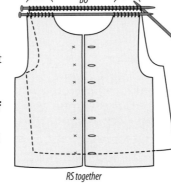

3 needle BO   BO   3 needle BO

RS together

Working the shoulder bind-off

Starting at one end of the shoulder and with right sides together, bind off the shoulder stitches using the three-needle bind-off, bind off the back neck stitches, and return to three-needle bind-off across the other shoulder (see illustrations).

Neck edges

Once the shoulders are joined, it is time to finish the neckline. Measure the distance around the neck edge and work using the information gathered from your crochet or knit.

Collar

A collar is often designed with the cast-on edge as its border and the bound-off edge to be sewn to the neckline. This is practical, because a bound-off edge has less give than a cast-on edge. To attach a collar, fold it in half to mark the center and pin it to the center back neck with the right side of the collar overlaying the right side of the jacket. The edges of the collar are placed an inch from the neck front edges, or right at the edges if buttonbands are added. Pin the collar bind-off edge at the neckline edge and sew it into the neckline as neatly as possible.

SEAMING

Seaming knits with slip stitch crochet is easy, flexible, and durable (see ill.). Seams finished in this manner have stability and are easy to correct if things go awry. This seam most resembles the shoulder (3-needle bind-off) seaming, and traditional bind-off. Do try it— it works.

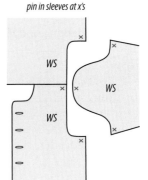

Setting in sleeves

Fold the armhole in half and mark the top of the shoulder. Then fold the sleeve cap in half and mark the middle point. Pin the two marks together with right sides facing each other. Pin the armhole edge to the sleeve edge on each side and ease the two fabrics together between these points. Slip stitch the armhole seam. Do not pull the stitches tightly; the seam should have some give. Check the right side of the work periodically to see how the seam looks and to make sure the design aligns properly. If not, pull out a few chain stitches and re-do them. Complete the seam (see ills.). Repeat for the opposite armhole

pin in sleeves at x's

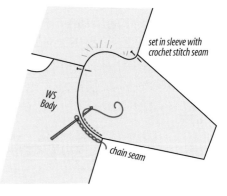

set in sleeve with crochet stitch seam

WS Body

chain seam

Sleeve and side seams

With the garment inside out (right sides facing each other), pin the edges of the sleeve together and the side front to the side back. Match the two ends of the armhole seam and slip stitch the seam from the armhole down to the hem, easing the fabric as necessary. Repeat the stitching for the sleeve, working from the armhole to the cuff. Continue to check the stitching to be certain the pattern aligns. (Remember, it's easy to undo the crochet seam if needed.) Again, do not pull the stitches too tightly; the seam should have some give (see illustration). Repeat for opposite side of jacket.

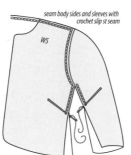

seam body sides and sleeves with crochet slip st seam

WS

CHANEL BRAIDS

Coco Chanel finished her jackets with a continuous trim around the back, front, and neck edges. This type of edge is applied after the jacket is assembled. Starting at the right side seam, work around the whole body edge and return to the starting point (see illustration). Work as many rounds as necessary to complete the edging, and fasten off. The join is least noticeable at a side seam.

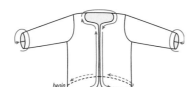

begin

FINAL TOUCHES

The jacket is now complete. Neaten the inside by sewing in and clipping ends. A final blocking or steaming will flatten the seams.

By applying these finishing techniques, your jacket will fit well, look fantastic, and rival anything you can purchase.

We know you will want to knit at least one, if not all of the wonderful jackets in this book. The perfect finishing touch to your jacket will be a beautiful label.

To receive 3 free labels contact us at:

label@xrx-inc.com

800-232-5648

XRX, Inc.
P.O. Box 1525
Sioux Falls, SD 57101

Now add your label!

also from XRX Books

Gerdine Strong
ANGELS: A KNITTER'S DOZEN

Susan Mills & Norah Gaughan
THE BEST OF LOPI

Priscilla A. Gibson-Roberts
ETHNIC SOCKS & STOCKINGS

Meg Swansen
A GATHERING OF LACE

Cheryl Potter
HANDPAINT COUNTRY

·KIDS·KIDS·KIDS·

Sally Melville
THE KNITTING EXPERIENCE:
BOOK 1 THE KNIT STITCH

Anna Zilboorg
MAGNIFICENT MITTENS

Jean Moss
SCULPTURED KNITS

The Best of Knitter's
SHAWLS AND SCARVES

·SOCKS·SOCKS·SOCKS·

Sally Melville
STYLES

The Best of Weaver's
FABRICS THAT GO BUMP

The Best of Weaver's
HUCK LACE

The Best of Weaver's
THICK 'N THIN

KNITTER'S Magazine

visit us online at
www.knittinguniverse.com

visit us online   www.knittinguniverse.com XIX

Join the knitters' support
network: KnitU listserve at
www.knittinguniverse.com